THE PRODIGAL WORLD

THE
PRODIGAL WORLD

Social Reconstruction from Spiritual Regeneration

FULTON J. SHEEN

Addresses Delivered in the Catholic Hour Program
Produced by the National Council of Catholic Men
DECEMBER 29, 1935, TO APRIL 12, 1936

✳ ✳ ✳

CLUNY
Providence, Rhode Island

CLUNY EDITION, 2025

This Cluny edition is a republication of *The Prodigal World*,
first published in 1936 by the National Council of Catholic Men.

For more information regarding this title
or any other Cluny Media publication,
please write to info@clunymedia.com, or to
Cluny Media, P.O. Box 1664, Providence, RI 02901

WWW.CLUNYMEDIA.COM

Cluny edition copyright © 2025 Cluny Media LLC

All rights reserved.

ISBN: 978-1685953904

Cover design by Clarke & Clarke
Cover image: Hans Baluschek, *City of Workers*,
1920, oil on canvas
Courtesy of Wikimedia Commons

CONTENTS

The Rebirth of a World — [1]

Spiritual Bankruptcy — [10]

The Last of the Enemies — [21]

The Dignity of Man — [31]

The Bread of the Father's House — [42]

The Fundamental Liberty — [50]

The Sense of Sin — [58]

The Return from Exile — [67]

Calvary and Sacrifice — [75]

The First Word — [84]

The Second Word — [91]

The Third Word — [99]

The Fourth Word — [108]

The Fifth Word — [116]

The Sixth Word — [124]

The Seventh Word — [131]

The Finding of the Lost — [141]

THE REBIRTH OF A WORLD

DELIVERED ON DECEMBER 29, 1935

WE ARE LIVING in perilous times when the hearts and souls of men are sorely tried. Never before has the future been so utterly unpredictable; we are not so much in a period of transition with belief in progress to push us on, rather we seem to be entering the realm of the unknown, joylessly, disillusioned, and without hope. The whole world seems to be in a state of spiritual widowhood, possessed of the harrowing devastation of one who set out on life's course joyously in intimate comradeship with another, and then is bereft of that companion forever.

And in all this confusion and bewilderment our modern prophets say that our economics have failed us. No! It is not our economics which have failed; it is man who has failed—man who has forgotten God. Hence no manner of economic or political readjustment can possibly save our civilization; we can be saved only by a renovation of the inner man, only by a purging of our hearts and souls; for only by seeking first the Kingdom of God and His Justice will all these other things be added unto us. That is the way

FULTON J. SHEEN

the world twenty centuries ago was saved from paganism and selfishness. And that is the way it will be saved again. In order to bring home this truth, recall briefly how our Lord saved the world once before, and thus learn how it can be saved once again.

Have you ever adverted to the striking fact that the political, economic, and social conditions of the world at the time our Lord was born into it were very much like they are today? Never before have two periods of history been so alike. For example, in those days there was an intense nationalism in Israel, and a haughty militarism in Rome. With Caesar there arose a kind of dictatorship which absorbed individual rights. Economically, there was exploitation of labor and the Servile State. Taxation was excessive and overpowering; Religion was on the decline; the Gentiles lost faith in their gods, and Israel had no prophet since the days of the Maccabees. Wealth was in the hands of the few; life was becoming more of a riddle, in which solitary hearts lost nerve, begot no songs and few children, became weary of old culture, afraid of new gods, of fate, of the stars above and the world beyond. As Virgil, who lived during those times, described it:

> Where wrong and right are blest,
> A world that teems with war, a world that reeks
> With countless crime, where evermore the plough

THE PRODIGAL WORLD

> Lacks its due honor, and the hind is forced
> Far from the desolate fields, and reaping hooks
> Are straightened into swords.

Into this world with its depression, its despair, and its despondency, God came. And He came to set men and their world right with God—not only their hearts and their souls, but even their business, their secular affairs, their governments, and their all. How did He do it? God solved the social, political, and economic problems of the world not by enunciating a new economic system; nor by instructing man in the ways of supply and demand; nor by a great piece of research which revealed the many aspects of their problem; nor even by giving to the world a formula for finances, trade agreements, armaments, slavery, imperialism, or war. He saved it from its ills by being born as a babe in the insignificant village of Bethlehem. That seemingly trivial incident which was so commonplace that the innkeeper refused a room to His Blessed Mother was the revolution that upset the world and the solution which gave it peace. Driven even off the face of the earth He came to save, His Mother sought refuge in a shepherd's cave, and there under the floor of the world was born Him who like Samson shook the pillars of the world to its very foundations, pulled down the already crumbling edifice, and built a new Living Temple in its place, where men might once more sing because they had found their God.

But you ask what has the birth of a God in the form of a babe to do with the social, political, and economic conditions of His day and our own? What possible relation could exist between a child in a manger of straw and Caesar on his throne of gold? The answer is: The birth of the Son of God in the flesh was the introduction into the historical world-order of a new life; it was a proclamation to the world that social reconstruction has something to do with spiritual regeneration; that nations can be saved only by the men in them being re-born to God as God is now being born to man. Once God entered the created order on the level of humanity and became part of the stream of history, He gave man a new strength from above; He gave Him a Divine Power along with human power. In a word, God became man in order that man might become Godlike. That is why Christ was born a babe—to teach us that deliverance from economic and social ills can be obtained only by a birth.

Humanity was tired mentally and exhausted spiritually; for four thousand years it had been making the great experiment of Humanism, and was now like a sick man who could not cure himself. It was in a state like unto our own world, which since the days of the Renaissance, has tried to build its civilization on the self-sufficiency of man without God. Mankind left to itself slowly sinks downward

THE PRODIGAL WORLD

and reverts to the type of Adam. The law of necessary progress is a myth. We have proof enough that people advanced in culture may degenerate into savages, as our boasted twentieth century civilization degenerated into the butchery of the World War; but no solitary example exists of a race of savages rising to the civilized state by their own development. Apart from an outside supernatural assistance society goes from bad to worse until deterioration is universal. Not evolution but devolution is the law of man without God, just as it is the law of the sunflower without the sun. With all of our boasted mechanical civilization a day might come when our modern towers of Babel would be as forgotten as the first, when Americans would cease to exist as a race as the Babylonians and Medes have ceased to exist, when Washington would be a contested locality like the capital of the Aztec civilization, and when the constitution of the United States would be the hopeless search of the world's archaeologists. Distant as it may seem, it is something which has happened a hundred times before and which may very well happen again.

Humanity cannot lift itself by its own bootstraps; there is no such thing as spontaneous generation; life does not come from crystals; poetry does not come from donkeys; international peace does not come from wars; social justice does not come from selfishness. With all our knowledge of chemistry we cannot make a human life in our laboratories

FULTON J. SHEEN

because we lack the unifying, vivifying principle of a soul which comes only from God. Life is not a push from below; it is a gift from above. It is not the result of the necessary ascent of man, but the loving descent of God. It is not the term of Progress; it is the fruit of the Incarnation. Hence; like that world into which Christ was born, the world today needs not a shuffling of old ideas, not a new economic, not a new monetary system—it needs a new birth. It needs the intrusion into our order of a new life and a new spirit, which God alone can give. We cannot give ourselves this new Birth any more than we can be born again naturally. If we are to be born again into the newness of life the regenerating principle must come from above, and that is precisely the meaning of the Incarnation: The introduction into the world on the level of human nature of the Life of God, who came not to judge the world, but to save it. And this is why I say He solved our problems by appearing as a Babe, because the regeneration of society has something to do with Birth.

Immediately you say: This is but theory; the Incarnation of the Son of God took place nineteen hundred years ago, and is just as past as the Battle of Waterloo. No! The Incarnation is not past. How can God belong to the past? The Incarnation is taking place *right now*. What God did to that individual human nature which He took from Mary His Mother is what He wills to do, in a lesser degree, to every human nature in the world; namely, to make us partakers of His divine life. He who from all eternity was born of the eternal Father was born in time in Bethlehem. He wills that we who are born in time of our earthly fathers, should be reborn in eternity of the heavenly Father, made new creatures, become possessed of new life, and members of the Kingdom of God. Let me make this clear by an example: When a government wishes to issue a coin, it first of all makes the original dye. This original model requires the work of a consummate artist. But once the dye is cast, the model formed, millions and millions of coins may be struck from it, each bearing the resemblance of the original. Now, Bethlehem is the city where the dye was struck and Christ Himself is the dye. All the men who have lived and will ever live are the raw material awaiting the stamp of the divine original. But in order to be like Him, that is, a sharer of His divine life, we must be struck off that dye. And the Baptismal font is the new Bethlehem where the copies are made, for there men are re-born again to the Life of God. O think not that Baptism means merely a sprinkling of water, as if you had no other eyes than those which are blinded by dust! Do you say money is only a mechanical product of a steel dye, or do you say it has a value because backed by the power of government?

Why then should we not say that Baptism is externally a cleansing, but internally it is a regeneration, and a new life, because backed by the Divinity of Christ? The incarnation is the Model and the Pattern, the Baptismal Font is its prolongation and extension; for in both a birth takes place: the birth of God in the flesh and the birth of the flesh in God. Now do you understand why God solved the economic, political, and social problems of His time by a birth—because man could never be saved except by being regenerated?

And that is the only way we can ever solve our economic, political, and social problems; namely by being re-born to that divine life; by being incorporated to Him who gives us a power above our will, a wisdom above our reason, and a strength above our arms. That same Divine Life that came into the world-process nineteen hundred years ago, must come back into it again. Unless we are born again—we shall perish. The barrier to our progress is our broken hearts and only Christ can give us a new heart. Our old hearts have hardened; our old minds are confused; our old habits overpower us. We need a fresh start, a new re-shaping, a new quickening spirit. And the more there are of us who are struck off the great original divine dye of Christ, the better the world will be. It is not economics which have failed us; it is man who has failed because he refuses to be signed with the sign of Christ. Economic reconstruction is therefore conditioned upon spiritual regeneration; our ills today are not political and

THE PRODIGAL WORLD

economic, but moral and religious; we are not going to be saved by finances or armaments, any more than the chosen people of God were saved by horsemen because they were many, or horses because they were strong. The Gospel of Spiritual Regeneration which alone can save us will be presented under the parable of the Prodigal Son, with which I shall begin next Sunday. It will not, I trust, be just a vague appeal to follow Christ; it will be an appeal to be re-born in Christ—to live spiritual lives, to be infused with divine life. The idea of re-birth is a happy one with which to begin the New Year. My wish to you is that you will have a Happy New Year—but by a new year I do not mean new in the sense of another; for if a new year were just another year it would not be so happy—there is no happiness in adding year to year and growing older. By a new year I mean new in the sense of regenerated, rejuvenated, new-born; for there is happiness in having life before you—especially the eternal life of God. Now you know how deep and heartfelt are my greetings when I say to you individually: I wish you a Happy New Year—God love you!

SPIRITUAL BANKRUPTCY

DELIVERED ON JANUARY 5, 1936

AS ANNOUNCED LAST SUNDAY the purpose of this course is to suggest that social reconstruction is conditioned upon spiritual regeneration, that our ills today are not fundamentally economic and political, but moral and religious. Hence if the world is ever to recover its lost social peace, it must once more find God.

This lesson—so important for our times—will be presented in the light of the parable of the Prodigal Son. Our Lord, you will recall, began the parable thus: "A certain man had two sons: And the younger of them said to his father: Father, give me the portion of substance that falleth to me. And he divided unto them his substance. And not many days after, the younger son, gathering all together, went abroad into a far country: and there wasted his substance, living riotously."

The interpretation we shall give of this parable is not moral but historical. The younger son in the parable is Western Civilization. After many long centuries in union with the Father's house, Western Civilization finally asked

THE PRODIGAL WORLD

the Spiritual Father for its share of inheritance—not inheritance in the form of gold and silver, but rather spiritual capital in the form of eternal truths necessary for salvation. Carried away by the new-found independence from the Father's House, Western Civilization began to spend the spiritual capital which the Father's House had given to it. The history of the last four centuries is very briefly the *history of that wasted capital*—the patrimony of Christ committed to His Church. It was not all spent at once, nor was it all spent in the same place, nor with the same friends. Century by century the substance became smaller and smaller, and now as we look back in history, we can tell when each part of the capital was spent. In the sixteenth century, Western civilization spent its belief in the necessity of authority. In the seventeenth century, it spent its belief in Sacred Scripture as the revealed word of God. In the eighteenth century, it spent its belief in the Divinity of Christ, the necessity of grace, and the whole supernatural structure. In the nineteenth century, it spent its belief in the existence of God as the Lord and Master, and the Supreme Judge of the living and the dead. And in our own day, it has spent its last penny—a belief in the necessity of religion and the obligation to a Personal God. Truly, indeed, it has wasted its spiritual capital living riotously.

The story of the last three hundred years is the story of a spiritual declension and the squandering of the substance

FULTON J. SHEEN

of Divine Truth. Christ, who is God, has been reduced to a mere man. Man, who is made to the image and likeness of God, has been reduced to a mere animal. And an animal, which is a living thing, has been reduced to a mere atom. And this is called "Progress"! Is it any wonder that thoughtful men are beginning to write and speak of the Decline of the West? Spengler, Massis, and a host of others, in making a retrospect of our Western World, are right in saying that it is on the decline. Many of them are wrong only in their explanation. It is not machinery, nor finance, nor naval armaments, nor the amassing of gold, nor rigorous iron laws of determinism, which have effected this decline. The two decisive factors in the breakdown of Western Civilization have been the two causes just mentioned—mass-defection from Christ and mass-defection from God.

Continuing the parable of the prodigal, our Lord tells us that "there came a mighty famine in that country; and he began to be in want." There is always a famine in a far-off land which means being away from the Father's House. Before the spirit is quite quenched and the soul wholly carnalized, there remains a craving for higher things; but when the spirit is quenched, and the soul is imbruted, there is a famine of even that false bread which is not bread, and a thirst for those stolen waters which only makes the thirst more keen. The hunger is now of such a kind that it can no longer taste the food of virtue. It is that queer after-taste of

THE PRODIGAL WORLD

all the world's feasts—a distaste for what we have, and an abhorrence of that which we have not. At one stroke our Lord set it before us, compressing into a single sentence the history of all erring souls, the fate of all sinful nations and all sinful men—"And he went and cleaved to one of the citizens of that country. And he sent him into his farm to feed swine. And he would fain have filled his belly with the husks the swine did eat; and no man gave unto him." "He would fain have filled his belly"—for it is no longer a question of satisfying his appetite, but only of satisfying the lower part of himself. Only God can satisfy the real hunger, for no one can feed the heart but God. The poor prodigal was now sitting beside the ashes of a palace which his own hands had burned. He was feeding on husks and he was still in want. It is a passage from ten thousand biographies.

Now to resume the interpretation of the prodigal son in the light of spiritual experience in the modern world. Leaving the father's house, Western Civilization gradually squandered its spiritual heritage, living well with the modern world, becoming popular with it by sacrificing some of the best of its spiritual possessions for the sake of a momentary applause. Having wasted its substance riotously, a famine now arises in the land. A famine not for bread of the body alone, but a famine for the bread of the spirit. Today, there is a famine for divine certainty and guidance among those who spent the capital of their belief

FULTON J. SHEEN

in Sacred Scripture; there is a famine for a helping hand more kindly than the human among those who spent belief in His Divinity; there is a famine for perfect life, truth, and love, among those who spent belief in the Trinity. Everywhere there is a famine for faith among those who doubt, a famine for God among those who substituted illusions for majestic faiths, and a famine for love amongst those who war. Everywhere there is a feeling of emptiness like that which follows a fever or an unhappy love affair.

"And he went and cleaved to one of the citizens of that country." Like the prodigal who, in the days of famine, cleaved to a citizen of the foreign country, so too does the religion of Western Civilization in the days of its spiritual famine attach itself to temporalities which are foreign to the service of God; it links itself up with things which are strange to religion, alien to the Kingdom of Heaven. Having lost divinity, modern religion now ties itself up to a thousand worldly interests which are not of the essence of religion, such as politics, social reform, economics, drug control, and opposition to the liquor traffic. It becomes in the language of a distinguished Professor of Yale, identified with national cultures, and hence devoid of all common reference to the Cross. I am not saying that religion should not be interested in the things of Caesar, nor that it should be indifferent to politics, nor that it should turn a cold shoulder to the opium problem; but I do say that these are

THE PRODIGAL WORLD

not the primary concern of religion nor that to which religion owes first allegiance, any more than it can be said that the prodigal owed greater allegiance to the citizen of a foreign country than to his own father. Religion is indeed in a foreign land when it is more interested in mental hygiene than in the forgiveness of sin; in politics more than prayer; in the book of Darwin rather than the book of Isaiah; in the theory of relativity rather than in the Absolute; in crime prevention rather than morals; and in sex more than God.

This sad and tragic dissipation of spiritual capital by the Western World does not necessarily mean the Decline of the West. There is still a possibility of recovery as there was for the Prodigal. What saved the Prodigal was the fact that he never became a citizen of the foreign country. He was always a stranger there. There would have been no hope for him, however, if he had not felt himself an alien, or if he had made himself a citizen in that land of husks. And so too with Western Civilization. Were it untroubled by heavenly homesickness, were there no divine nostalgia, no remembrance of a Father's House, there would be no hope. But such is not the case. There is a feeling of being a stranger in this land which has forgotten the Divine; there is a feeling of uneasiness, a discontent with the husks it is given, and a yearning for the food which nourishes unto life everlasting.

Up until the World War one could not pick up a book,

FULTON J. SHEEN

or a magazine, or listen to a speech, without hearing something about "Progress." Everywhere there was hope, prosperity—a certain onward, upward march to the tune of evolution, to the Golden Age of material prosperity and earthly happiness.

Then came the World War which turned the world into a slaughterhouse. The so-called civilized man, who was supposed to be a descendant of the ape, now acted like one. The great Babels of earthly happiness built without the great Cornerstone, came tumbling down on our heads. Visions of grandeur began to fade. And then came the Depression. The machine which was to make us all rich and happy made many poor and miserable. It produced more than the men which it displaced could buy. The world had hoped for peace, and it got wars and rumors of wars; it was promised prosperity, and got starvation in the midst of plenty; it had hoped to make the world safe for democracy, and got a democracy which was hardly safe for the world; it was promised a world free from authority and got tyrannical dictatorship. The result is that today instead of Progress, Evolution, Prosperity, and World Peace, we have decay, unrest, uncertainty, doubt, and above all else a feeling of not knowing where we are going. Man now crouches in fear from the very terrors he himself has created. He has set fire to his own house and now it tumbles involving him in its ruins. And that whole school of false prophets who once

THE PRODIGAL WORLD

talked Progress are now resigned to a philosophy which is hardly distinguishable from despair. The map was thrown aside and the world has lost its way.

But there is no reason for despair. However much Western Civilization has been disillusioned, it still feels itself in a foreign land. There is still some remembrance of the Father's House. Suffice it to say here that some are coming back again to God, not through the preservation of their baptismal grace, but by a trial of the world. They are dissatisfied in this foreign land of husks. They have leaned on the staff of the economic and secular and found it pierced their hands. Like the Prodigal, they are witnessing against the world, even though they are children of it. It is a great mercy that those having lost the free gift of God can regain it by His compulsory remedies; and who after having heard all the ramblings of skeptics and tasted the fleeting pleasures of an hour, now are made to cry out with Peter at Capernaum, "Lord, to whom shall we go?"

It may take a long time for Western Civilization to realize that the good it is seeking is the good that it left. Many heart-aches and long sad experiences were necessary before the Prodigal realized that the father's house which he left was the only place he could find freedom, peace, and contentment. In like manner the world will not quickly realize that the Church which it believed was so restraining to liberty is really the only force that can make us free, and

FULTON J. SHEEN

that that which was so much behind the times is the only institution which has survived the times.

However long the time it takes to learn the lesson, there is always the consoling picture of the father of the prodigal who daily would mount a hill and look down all the roads to the foreign land hoping almost against hope that he would catch a glimpse of his son. So too the spiritual Father of all Christendom is daily mounting one of the seven hills of Rome from which one can look down all the roads that lead to Rome; daily his eyes search the horizons of the foreign land for Western Civilization that is already dying of famine for the things of the Spirit of God.

The Church has not been tried for three hundred years; it has not even been considered; it has only been *ignored*. The world knows less about her than about the man in the moon. It has never studied her claims, never searched out her secrets; and it dispenses itself from doing so for the same reason the first hearers of Christ dispensed themselves from hearing His message: "Can anything good come out of Nazareth?" Ignorance can be accumulated just as well as wisdom, and during the last three hundred years the world has accumulated a tremendous amount of ignorance concerning her. Through long centuries she has been outlawed and ignored, but she has never failed any more than Christ failed when His fellow citizens cast Him out of

THE PRODIGAL WORLD

His hometown of Nazareth. Her days of being ignored are over. She is now returning from exile. The exile has been good for her. It has permitted the world to distinguish her from her imitators; it has been a lesson to her not ever to become worldly again: it has allowed the blood to run back again to her heart to energize her for the reconversion of the world. Even if there are some who hate, they must be excused for they do not really hate the Church, but only what they mistakenly believe to be the Church. The vision of the Church will come to them as one awakened in the watches of the night; they will see the dead walking and the blaze of that living death will make them forget everything else but the glory of the Risen Christ.

Let us not be misled into believing that a new religion, such as a pot-pourri of Eastern and Western religion, will arise to satisfy the cry of the world. The human heart that has had one great love can never really have another. We have but one heart and if we give it away, we give away our deepest capacity for love. What is true of the individual is true of society. Society has used up a life's capacity for love in the great adventure of Christianity. Its bones are too old to accustom themselves to new postures of worship. We have given our heart away once to the Divinity of the Church—we cannot give it away again.

That is why the world will end as Christianity began—with a great and mighty battle between the world and the

FULTON J. SHEEN

Church, between Baal and Christ, between the forces who crucify and the Power which is crucified.

THE LAST OF THE ENEMIES

DELIVERED ON JANUARY 12, 1936

WESTERN CIVILIZATION may be likened to the Prodigal Son in that it has left the Father's house and wasted its substance living riotously by spending its belief in the supernatural and even the natural end of man.

A fragment, of course, of that spiritual capital is still floating about the world, for, to change the figure, our age is living in what might be called the penumbra of Christianity—that line where light fades out and shadows begin. All that is still sublime in philanthropy is but a splinter of the Cross of Calvary which the Church holds erect above the world; all that is noble and happy in marriage is a reflection from the marriage feast of Cana and the Church's teaching of the sanctity of two hearts and the honesty of a vow; all that is best in the justice and equity of governments is a reflection of the Church's spiritual principle that we must render unto Caesar the things that are Caesar's and unto God the things that are God's; and all that is satisfying in democracy is the principle that all are equal because redeemed by the precious blood of Our Savior, Jesus Christ.

FULTON J. SHEEN

But apart from this reflection of Christian truth which is still dimly visible in the world, the great spiritual patrimony of the ages is gone. The Church with her finger on the pulse of contemporary civilization realizes it more than our moribund civilization itself realizes it. Humanism has failed. The Church feels the shift of the opposition. Western Civilization is not just suffering from a famine of spiritual values; it is not even caring about them. It is now seeking to "fill its belly"; namely, to stuff itself with the husks of the secular, the economic, the political, the worldly. And the name of this new thing which no longer is concerned with the soul but with the belly is Communism, the new enemy of the Father's House and probably the last. Communism is not merely an economic doctrine. It is more properly a philosophy of life which mobilizes souls for economic and secular ends; a Caesarism or adoration of the State; a glorification of the human collective through the de-personalization of men; a suffocation of human personality and its subsequent absorption into the mass; a filtering of barbarism through the sieve of the class, the race, or the state, and calling it Civilization.

It is not peculiar to Russia alone. We see there mobilization of souls under an economic disguise where one hundred and sixty million of God's creatures destined for eternal life are dehumanized and reduced to the state of ants whose sole business in life is to build up the great ant-hill of

THE PRODIGAL WORLD

the Classless Class; we see it in Mexico with a political disguise where treason is synonymous with the worship of the Crucified; we see it with a racial mask in Germany where the State would crush the Religion of Him who rose from the dead, and would return to the barbarism of gods who are still rotting in their graves. In all three instances men are bludgeoned into living their lives without God; they are beaten and hammered into the new pattern where the gods of economics are supreme.

How has this world movement of the mobilization of souls for secular ends come upon us? One reason is, the World War accustomed us to mobilization, and as a consequence to the relative unimportance of man. When a world which boasts of its progress reaches a point where it can send millions of men *en masse* into a battlefield, to make rivers run red, to turn poppy fields into Haceldamas of blood, to tear great gaping wounds in Gothic cathedrals, it has indeed forgotten that every man has an immortal soul, and in the eyes of God is just as personal and as valuable as the King who declares a war, or the General who directs it behind the lines, and even more valuable if he loves God more. The inalienable and sacred rights of human personality are indeed regarded as trivial, when the bones of six million men can be strewn across the fields for a cause which is still unknown. Creatures of God have lost their importance when they can be generalized with the

FULTON J. SHEEN

anonymous title: "The Unknown Soldier." That war spirit of mobilization which resulted in mass suicide—for that is what the World War was—has left its imprint on the modern mind. The world is still mobilizing, still ignoring the human, still counting bodies instead of souls, still thinking of poverty instead of the poor and of the masses instead of man.

Communism is not new except in the sense that a decaying corpse is a new state in relation to a living man. It was not a revolution which began a new epoch; it was a revolution which marks the death of an old one; it is not a cry of birth, it is the rattle of death; it is not a new blossom on a new vine, it is the late season fruit of the tree of spiritual bankruptcy. It takes a branch cut off from the vine some time to die, but eventually it dies. Communism is that death—it is the logical development of a civilization which for the last three hundred years has lived its economic life without God.

It is therefore not a reaction against Capitalism but the glorification of its worst features, and the ignoring of its better features. The old Capitalism made the economic the principal basis of civilization. Communism makes it the *unique* basis of civilization. The old Capitalism wanted no interference from the state but left God and religion alone provided they did not interfere. The new Capitalism, or Communism, says: If the supreme business of life is to subjugate man to the economic order, to mechanize human life, then why not make the economic order not the end of the individual but the very end of the State itself? Therefore no longer entrust the mad pursuit of the secular and the economic to a group of individuals, or to a few scattered capitalists. Make the economic the end of everyone. Force it down the throats of everyone; jam it into their souls and suffocate the thought of God; cram it into their hearts and extinguish the fires of Divine Love. The State itself shall be Capitalist! The State itself shall seek Wealth! The Economic shall be the end of man!

Why is Communism growing in popularity? It is popular because the modern man is tired of selfish individualism, is satiated with a democracy that follows the public will, instead of leading it. He feels the need of a reaction; he wants something that will help him return to the center of his being; he wants the spiritual or at any rate something over which he can enthuse; he wants something different from anything he has had in the last three hundred years: and since the only Christianity he knows is that emasculated form of it which regards Christ only as man, and which has identified itself with the social order that is passing away, he feels that Christianity has failed. And so the modern man turns to Communism. He seeks it because it replaces the doubt and skepticism of an irresponsible indifference by a certitude of absolute authority embodied in a

FULTON J. SHEEN

social institution; he seeks it because he believes it will save the world; he seeks it because he wants a logical system that lays claim to his body and soul. In a word he is a Communist because it satisfies his need of religion.

Communism is a religion. This is its positive side. But it is not just a religion in the sense that Humanism is a religion, or even Confucianism is a religion. Communism is not a heresy within the body of Christendom, rather it is the ape of Christianity in its divine and historical form. It has not taken one of the truths of Christianity and emphasized it, as most erroneous forms of Christianity have done in the last three hundred years. Rather it has taken the whole content of Christianity and given it a new soul. It has changed Christianity in the same way that man would be changed if you robbed him of his immortal soul and gave him the soul of a serpent. The man would see, taste, smell, and in general carry on all the vegetative and animal functions common to the body of every man. Externally he would even appear as other men; but on the inside he would be different. And why? Because he would lack a rational soul which is capable of lifting him above the fleeting phenomena of earth to a knowledge and love of the living God.

Communism has its Bible, which is *Das Kapital* of Karl Marx; it has its original sin which is Capitalism; it has its chosen people which is the Classless Class; it has its Messianic hope which is the World Proletariat; it has its "Sermon on the Mount" which is its false appeal to the poor and oppressed; it has its monasticism which is the infiltration of its doctrines through the "cells"; it has its Gospel which is the Gospel of Class War; it has its communion of saints which is the comradeship of man; it has its Calvary which is an appeal to sacrifice oneself for the Communistic state; it has its Kingdom of God but without God and of the earth earthly; it lays claim to absolute truth which no politics or economics can claim; it has its catechism which is obligatory on everyone; it has its orthodoxy and it persecutes its heretics; it lays claim to the very depths of the soul, possessing the conscience and the spirit of man—and only a religion can do this. It persecutes all religions because it claims to be the one true religion and hence can suffer no other; it is the religion of the Kingdom of Earth, the religion which renders to Caesar even the things that are God's; it is the body of the elect, the new Israel, the ape of Christianity in all externals. It differs only in its soul, for its spirit is the spirit of the serpent; it is the Mystical Body of Anti-Christ.

Thus far we have emphasized the idea that Communism is not just a system of economics but a philosophy of life; and that it is the logical development of a civilization which for three hundred years has built its political, economic, and social structure without the solid foundation of the regnancy of God in human affairs.

FULTON J. SHEEN

Now go on to inquire how it can be met. Because it is something social and communal it cannot be met by any shouting for rugged individualism; it can be met only by something social, communal. Because it expresses a longing for a real community of men, it can be met only by a community where personality is not extinguished, where the soul is not killed, but allowed to flower and blossom in that higher realm of Life and Truth and Love which is God.

Because Communism is a religion which makes the State a god and the factory a place of pilgrimage, it can be met only by a religion which serves the State by serving God. World peace can be recovered only by a spiritual force which avoids the two extremes of Individualism and Communism; a force which asserts against Individualism that man cannot live apart from society; and one which equally asserts against Communism that a person has rights to worship God which the State cannot take away; a force that is not the technical organized force of Communism, but the spiritual organic force which mobilizes souls for eternal ends—and that it is the historical form of Christianity which has been excluded from Civilization for the last three hundred years and which is now returning from exile, namely, the Church. Communism has only one enemy: The Eternal Galilean. The Mystical Body of the State can be conquered only by the Mystical Body of Christ.

THE PRODIGAL WORLD

Such is the method our Lord chose to regenerate a world; namely through a spiritual community in which He became, as it were, "incarnate." The Church therefore is to save the world by being in it, but not of it; it is to be a city set on a hill toward which men may turn their eyes to know the secret of their strength, but it is not the hill; it is to be a light shining out through the darkness of a troubled world, but it is not the darkness; it is to be a leaven in the dead mass of sin-stained humanity, but it is not the mass; it is to be the salt wherewith the earth is to be salted, but it is not the earth. Above all else, it is a fellowship, a spiritual Communism, based not on the laws of society, nor the ties of blood nor the necessities of economics, but on the re-ordering of the whole field of human relations in a spirit of charity, and a cohesion of shattered and despised mankind under the leadership of Christ. The world will be saved from Communism and the martyrdom of man only by this society whose basic inspiration is the primacy of spiritual values: "Seek ye first the kingdom of God and His justice, and all these things shall be added unto you." The Mystical Body of Christ alone can oppose the Mystical Body of Anti-Christ.

These are the only two complete philosophies of life: The Church and Communism. The future conflicts of the world will not be between Religion and Science, or between "rugged individualism" and Socialism, but between a

FULTON J. SHEEN

society which is spiritual and a society which is mechanical, between a society which adores God and a society which claims it is god. No more civil wars; from now on an invasion. The world must make the choice. The forces are already aligning themselves for the battle. We must enlist on one side or the other; we must battle either for brotherhood in Christ or comradeship in anti-Christ. The prodigals will either come back to Christ or they will go the way of all flesh and fill their bellies with the economic and the secular. The world of the future will have only two capitals, Moscow and Rome; it will have only two temples, the Red Square and St. Peter's; only two sanctuary lamps, the Red Flag and the red glow of the Eucharistic lamp; only two tabernacles, the Kremlin and Emmanuel; only two hosts, the rotted body of Lenin and the Body of the Living Christ; only two hymns, the Internationale and the Panis Angelicus—but only *one victory*, the victory of the Captain Christ bearing five wounds in the forefront of battle.

THE DIGNITY OF MAN

DELIVERED ON JANUARY 19, 1936

THE INTERPRETATION of the parable of the prodigal son in our broadcasts up to this point has been this: The younger son may be likened to Western Civilization which left the Father's House and squandered its spiritual capital of eternal religious truth. It finally sank so low that it would fain have filled its belly with husks; and this philosophy which fills bellies and mobilizes souls for secular ends is Communism. The choice before the world is between a philosophy which makes society a god, and a society which seeks God.

Today, we begin the inquiry into the first of the four conditions which civilization must fulfill if it is to recover peace and salvation. Returning to the parable for our guide, it will be recalled that while the prodigal was delighting in his new-found pleasures and false liberty, there was very little thought of his spiritual destiny. It is a very interesting thing that he did not begin to reflect until he was reduced to dire need and misery. Our Blessed Lord speaks first of the return of the prodigal in these expressive words: "He entered into himself." This implies that up to this time he was "outside himself," or "beside himself"; i.e., all his enjoyments were something external to himself: such as food, pleasure, and dance, and in general what some men call "life." In this he was like the beasts of the field, for they seek things outside of themselves. The animal in quest of food and the flower lifting its face to the sun, the bird dipping for the worm—all of these have no other end or purpose in life than some object outside themselves. They can never enter into themselves, for the very simple reason that they have no rational soul. Man is the only being in the world who can reflect, and hence the only one who can turn back upon himself, be angry with himself, be pleased with himself, contemplate his own thoughts, perceive the difference between what he is and what he seems, between his own worth and what others attribute to him. He is the only creature in the universe who can look upon himself as in a mirror, and see himself as others see him, and even sit, as it were, on another planet and let his feet hang over, contemplating off in the distance another person which happens to be his very self.

Now to continue the historical application of the parable: Civilization will return to peace and order when it "enters into itself"; i.e., reflects upon the end and purpose of being a man. We cannot talk of building a social or economic order for man, unless we know the purpose of a man, any more than an architect can build a house unless he knows the nature of the one to dwell in it. If a dog is to live in it, it will be a dog house; if a criminal is to live in it, it will be a penitentiary; if a Malthusianite is to live in it, it will have no nursery. In like manner, the kind of social order we will build will depend upon the nature of the man for whom it is made. If he is only an economic animal, then we will let Communism give him a bed in a factory; but if he is a rational creature, made to the image and likeness of God, then we will have to build something else besides a factory for him; e.g., a house which will be a home, a school which will be the arsenal of truth for his children, and a church where his soul can escape the servitude of the earthly and mount to eternal union with God.

Hence, I say the *fundamental* problem facing civilization today is not the problem of unemployment, nor finance, nor free trade, nor gold standards, nor even property rights. The problem of the hour is the problem of man. What is a man? Is he an economic animal, or is he a rational creature composed of body and soul, and capable of entering into communion with the triple environment which surrounds him, namely, nature, fellowman, and God? The way we answer the problem of man is the way we will solve our social problem.

Two powerful influences in our civilization have done much to degrade, mechanize, and depersonalize man, and

FULTON J. SHEEN

keep him from entering into himself. The first is false economics, which says that the primary end of business is not consumption, but production. Start with this principle and it follows then that the purpose of a machine is not to supply human needs, but to make profit for its owner. The price then becomes more important than the *man* who pays the price. It is then only a step to say that the produce of God's bountiful land may be destroyed in the midst of starvation for the sake of an economic price. Man becomes subordinate to economics, instead of economics to man, and this means a degradation and impoverishment of human dignity.

Secondly, a false education is to be blamed for destroying the true nature of man. A bad psychology told man he had no soul, then no mind, and finally no consciousness, but that he was only a complex machine made up of actions and reactions, ganglia and glandoozings. Biology told him he was evolving to the state of a god, then Physics contradicted this and told him that in view of the greatness of the universe he was only a "crustal phenomenon floating on an insignificant planet." Robbed of God by the error that God was only a symbol for "the ideal tendency in things"; robbed of will by the behaviorist and gland psychology; robbed of his intellect by theories of knowledge which doubted his capacity to know; robbed of his soul by the subconscious, the subliminal, and sex—he became

THE PRODIGAL WORLD

only an atom dissolved in the mass of a two-dimensional universe of space and time, with no other purpose than like an ant to pile his contribution of economic wealth on the great ant-hill of the State and then to die and to be seen no more. Such is the end of the Renaissance which began by exalting man without God and ended by slaying both.

These are the two forces which destroyed traditional man, and sought to break the mould in which God poured him. They have created for our times the problem stated so clearly in the parable, namely, whether man is to seek material things wholly outside himself, like husks, or to enter into himself and recognize his eternal destiny. This problem must be solved before any economic problem can be solved, for what is the use of constructing an economics for man unless we know the nature of man? The problem of man must be solved first because it is on his account that the social problem must be solved. When the world was living on the spiritual capital given to it by the Church, systems of economics and government and finance acknowledged the true nature of man. But now that the nature of man is challenged, and human personality is absorbed by the state as in Russia, Mexico, and Germany, and when economic rights precede human rights, the problem of man must be settled first. And if it is not settled, then all our solutions will fail, for souls are being born into the world every minute, presenting the riddle all over again.

FULTON J. SHEEN

Our problem today then is the problem of the Forgotten Man—not the forgotten man in the sense of the man who is unemployed, or hungry; not the forgotten man who is economically dispossessed, or socially disinherited; not the forgotten man of the bread lines, but forgotten man in the sense of forgotten human dignity, forgotten human worth, forgotten divine destiny, forgotten personality, forgotten power to rise above the state and the collective to commune with the Life and Truth and Love which is God. This is the real Forgotten man of our day—the man who can enter into himself and find down in the depths of his soul that he was made for God and only God can make him remembered—even for eternity.

Now, we ask, how can a prodigal civilization rediscover its last harmony? Only in the same way the prodigal son discovered his, namely by entering into itself; i.e., by recognizing the simple but forgotten principle that man has a final end. One of the first questions in the penny catechism is: "Why did God make you? God made me to know Him, to love Him, to serve Him in this world and to be happy with Him forever in the next." These words which sum up the wisdom of Aristotle and St. Thomas and the best thought of the world, both pre-Christian and Christian, are worth more than all our modern prophets who have not yet discovered why they are men. They reveal that this world is a stage of character-making wherein all our actions have

THE PRODIGAL WORLD

tremendous consequences; where happiness like art must be won by effort, by struggle and practice; where a soul is at stake in the living of a human life, for we are not only creatures but creatures of our eternal destiny. This fundamental concept of rational and moral relations between God and man involving the eternal happiness of man with God, must penetrate the whole of life. At every moment from birth to death man is envisaged as seeking the realization of the "ought to be." For this end he has been placed here. Hence none of his actions is insignificant; nothing is indifferent, nothing is trivial; everything he does, thinks, or chooses brings him nearer his goal or away from it. According to this philosophy every economic, political act of man is in a certain sense a religious and moral act. Man's final end is God and all proximate ends must keep this in mind. But once God as the goal or purpose of life is lost there is nothing left but skepticism and pessimism and a complete conversion to the earthly things which is the *sign of mortal sin*. It was just such a blindness to the final end of man which produced our modern cry that "business is business," implying that ethics and morality and religion have nothing to do with business. Business is *not* business—business is either *good* business or *bad* business, and it is good or bad because it helps or does not help man to attain his final destiny which is God. Forget the ultimate destiny of man and a new god will be created for him—a cruel god, which is the tyrannical State, as modern history is so well proving. When Rome forgot its religion it deified its emperors; when Western Civilization forgets its Christianity it begins to deify the State. This is Communism, the Moloch devouring men who forgot they had an immortal eternal tryst with undying Love who is God.

But once start with the true dignity of man, namely, by recognizing that he has a final end; that he is a personality living his complete life in society with obligations to his neighbor and to God; and finally that this world is only a prelude to the next—then we shall have the basis of true social reconstruction. Then "production is on account of man and not man on account of production, then the object of profit is that a man may provide for himself and for others according to their state, then the object of providing for himself and others is that they may be enabled to live virtuously. The object of the virtuous life is the attainment of everlasting glory with God." Then the world instead of being the storehouse of our mounded dust, becomes the scene of our greatest victory; then wealth is not something to *acquire*, but something to be used to increase virtue; then man becomes primary and economics secondary; then the material is the channel of the spiritual, and the universe becomes one great scaffolding up which souls climb to the Kingdom of God—and when the last soul shall have climbed up through that scaffolding then it shall be torn

THE PRODIGAL WORLD

down and burnt with fervent fire, not because it is bare, but because it has done its work—it has brought us back to where we started—the very heart of God.

In conclusion, if we doubt that the problem of man is primary, then let it be recalled that never before in the history of the world has there been so much power and never before have men been so prepared to use that power for the destruction of human life; never before has there been so much gold, and never before has there been so much poverty; never before has there been so much wealth, and never before has there been such an economic crisis; never before has there been so much food, and never before has there been so much starvation; never before have there been so many facts and never before have there been so many unsolved problems; never before has there been so much education, and never before has there been so little coming to the knowledge of truth. It is therefore not the material and the economic which has failed us, but the moral and religious inspiration to direct our material resources for the common good and the glory of God. This does not mean that there must not be political and economic and financial solutions; but it does mean these are *secondary*, and that they cannot be ultimately attained until we have "entered into ourselves" and discovered the end and purpose of being a man. This does not mean that anyone who interests himself in political and economic

FULTON J. SHEEN

matters has played false to the Kingdom of God; but it does mean that while due weight must be given to mass legislation as an instrument of reform, these things can be accomplished only by bringing God's breath upon the face of the earth. As Leo XIII stated in his *Rerum Novarum*: "The things of earth cannot be understood or valued aright without taking into consideration the life to come, the life that will know no death."

The note of this encyclical is: Spiritual and moral regeneration is the condition of political and economic reconstruction. Both economics and politics are doomed to unreality and failure unless grounded on the recognition that man is a spiritual being with ideals beyond this world. To recommend only political and economic panaceas for the world problem of dehumanized forgotten man, is like recommending face powder for someone suffering from jaundice, or an alcohol rub for someone suffering from cancer. It is not our bodies that are ill; the soul of civilization is sick. The world is in a state of mortal sin and it needs absolution. Vain platitudes about "regeneration," "the Constitution," and "progress," are not going to save us even though we do go on shouting them louder and louder. We need a new word in our vocabulary—and that word is God. We need a new standard of judging men than by the wealth they acquire, and that is the virtues they practice. We need less emphasis on the Five Year Plan and more on the Eternal Plan, for what doth it profit a man if he fill the world with tractors and lose his immortal soul?

THE BREAD OF
THE FATHER'S HOUSE

DELIVERED ON JANUARY 26, 1936

THE FIRST CONDITION of the prodigal's return to the Father's house was self-examination. The prodigal "entered into himself," that is, he began to do the pre-eminently human thing which differentiates him from the beast, namely, to reflect. The second condition revealed by the parable, was a recognition of a "sense of need." "How many hired servants in my father's house abound with bread, and I here perish with hunger." The misery, want, and spiritual desolation he felt in a foreign land made the prodigal yearn once again to break and eat the bread of the father's house.

If Western Civilization is to recover it must fulfill both these conditions. The first condition has already been discussed: It must enter into itself, i.e., respect the true nature of man. Now we pass on to the second condition which is a feeling of need; for unless it feels its own inadequacy, its own insufficiency, its own hunger, how can it aspire or even yearn for the Bread of the Father's house? There is no hope for any civilization which is hungry and does not wish for bread; but there is hope for one that is hungry and

THE PRODIGAL WORLD

feels the need of it. There is very apt to be in the minds of my hearers a general feeling that the Bread of the Father's House or the Eucharist is too spiritual a concept and can therefore have no application to the ills of our day. If we have any such suspicion it is only because we have lost hold of the fundamental truth that there is no salvation apart from God. In order to show how vital the Eucharist is to our problems, let us begin by contrasting the Capitalistic, the Communistic, and the Eucharistic or Catholic, philosophies of life.

The problem of social reconstruction revolves about the three words which have rung around the world since the French Revolution: "Liberty," "Equality," and "Fraternity." With which shall we begin? Which shall be first in rebuilding the social order? Capitalism said, Start with Liberty: Let a man be free, and let freedom mean the power to amass wealth without any interference either from the State, or the Church. Well, they had their liberty, which was only another word for selfishness, and it brought neither Equality nor Fraternity. Communism believes in starting with Equality, or the development of a homogeneous jelly-like state in which all men are equal because all are servants of the New Capitalism or Communism. They have had their "Equality," which was another name for tyranny, and it destroyed both Liberty and Fraternity. The Church says both are wrong. She says you cannot start with either

FULTON J. SHEEN

Liberty or Equality; you must start with Fraternity or Brotherhood. Brothers may share, but sharing does not make them brothers—that is the mistake of Communism. Thieves may share their loot, but such equality is only the equality of gangdom and not a brotherhood. In Russia, where there are no classes, the workers in a tractor factory and the O.G.P.U. are equal in the eyes of the State, but it is ridiculous to say they are brotherly.

There is only one way to build up a social order where men are free and equal and that is by starting with Brotherhood. There is only one way in the world to make men brothers, and that is by giving them a common body and a common blood. And there is only one Father in the universe who is good enough and powerful enough to make us all His adopted sons, and that is the Heavenly Father who so loved the world that He sent His Beloved Son into the world to give us His Body and His Blood.

Thanks to the Eucharist, the age-long symbol of the common meal becomes the basis of the brotherhood of men and the Fatherhood of God. Just as many grains of wheat make one bread, and many grapes of the vine make one wine, so we who are many are all made one in that Bread which is the Body and that Wine which is the Blood. Once men are made brothers of Christ and sons of the Heavenly Father at the Communion rail, then Equality and Liberty follow. Then men are both equal and free: *Equal*

THE PRODIGAL WORLD

because God loves each infinitely, and because each has a common need which God alone can supply; *free* because each soul is one with Christ who can do all things that are good—and what greater freedom is there than this?

The Communion rail is for that reason the most democratic institution on the face of the earth; it is even a greater leveler than death, for there the distinction between the rich and poor, the learned and unlearned disappears; there the millionaire must take the paten from the common laborer, the employer must kneel at the same board as the employee, the university professor must eat the same Bread as the simple Irishwoman who knows only how to tell her beads. There the dividing wall between nationalities is broken down and rebuilt into that spiritual Kingdom where all are one, because of One Lord, One Faith, One Baptism, One Bread. There every prayer is said in the great context of a brotherhood where every selfish act of the rich, and every envious deed of the poor, is envisaged as a hindrance to the unity of that Body. Hence, the real way to be a Communist is to be a Communionist or Communicant, i.e., to bring our hearts to the anvil of Divine Life and have them under the flames and fires of the Eucharist forged into that unity where we call one another not the atomic name of "Comrade" but the spiritual name of "Brother."

The beautiful superiority of the Eucharistic Life over the Capitalistic and Communistic views, thus emerges

FULTON J. SHEEN

because of the value it sets upon a man. Capitalism considered every man a "hand," and hence employers were wont to speak of having ten thousand "hands" in the factory; the newer Capitalism, or Communism, considers every man a "stomach" to be fed like the beast of the field, as long as he works to amass wealth for the great Capitalistic State. The Church, on the contrary, says man is neither a hand nor a stomach, but a creature composed of body and soul, made unto the image and likeness of God, and destined one day like the planets to complete his orbit and return unto that same God of Love who made him. The Church has ever insisted that mobilization must not minimize the value of a soul; and that collectivity does not make even a single soul less precious. Millions may go to war wearing only a tag, hundreds of thousands may go into factories with only a number, or may swell the breadlines under the generic title of "the unemployed," but for the Church each of these souls is just as precious in the sight of God as the soul of a Shakespeare or a Washington. And why is each man precious? Because God has paid an infinite price for him, namely the Blood of the Lamb slain from the beginning of the World.

However low he may sink, man is still in the eyes of the Church an exile from the royal household of God; for the King has issued the command: "Go out quickly into the streets and lanes of the city, and bring in hither the poor, and feeble, and the blind, and the lame." Or to paraphrase

THE PRODIGAL WORLD

it: Call in the hungry tramps, the beggars sleeping under papers on park benches, the sandwich-men placarding on their broken frames the latest luxuries, the sidewalk artists awaiting the drop of a penny, the half-nourished bodies crowding the out-patient wards of hospitals, the off-scouring of the earth, the broken earthenware of humanity—call them in, all of them! And these same souls who a moment before would have thought a bread line a Paradise and who would have picked a crust of bread from the gutter, call them in, tell them they have an immortal soul, sit them down at the Banquet of the King and nourish their souls with the Bread of Life and the Wine that germinates virgins. Judge them not by the clothes they wear, their accent or their knowledge of world affairs. Give them Divine Life, for their souls have need of life as well as their bodies. Tell them they are not just men, but children of God; infuse their peasant blood with the Blood of Royalty; rejuvenate their hungry bodies with the meat which nourishes unto life everlasting; lift them up from the slavery and serfdom of the world to the aristocracy of the family of the Trinity: let them forget for the moment their relations to the State, to the family, to society. Let each soul stand naked, face to face with God in a private audience with Divinity, where spirit meets Spirit, so that each may rise from the tryst as a new creature conscious that he must be worth something since God loves him so!

FULTON J. SHEEN

The real way then to establish the Classless Class is not by hatred and class-struggle, but by love and communion. Men are not called to be pessimists shouting and shrieking that life is too short, because it does not give man a chance to finish his Five Year Plan; they are called to be optimists rejoicing that Life is long enough to complete their part of the Eternal Plan. Souls are not so many sticks to be thrown into the great cosmic bonfire to keep it blazing for the next generation—each one is cut from the great quarry of humanity, and then squared and fitted as a Living Statue into the Temple of God by the Hand of the Heavenly Architect whose name is Love. This is the goal of life—union with God.

Does the Bread of the Father's House seem too idealistic? Do you condemn it because it is impractical? Certainly it is impractical, but that is precisely why it will succeed. When a machine is half out of order any tinker can fix it, but when it has gone radically wrong you need something more than a practical man. And so it is with the world today. It is too far gone for practical solutions. Its soul is sick!

Did not our Lord Himself choose a very impractical way to redeem and transform the world? Extremely impractical it was to put down economic and political injustices by dying on a cross! Impractical indeed it was to win a victory over the hardened hearts of men by going down to defeat!

THE PRODIGAL WORLD

Impractical indeed it was to save a selfish world by the Love which lost a day! No wonder the practical-minded men and women of His day when He was unfurled as a wounded eagle on the gibbet of the Cross, came beneath it and challenged Him to come down. "Come down from your Cross of impracticality. Come down and shake dice for the garments of a God; come down from your Cross of Love to our class struggle and our hate; come down from your love of God to a love of Caesar. The only man who will ever save us is the practical man who in the language of the commercially-minded has 'both feet on the ground.' But you have not both feet on the ground! You are suspended between heaven and earth, rejected by the one and abandoned by the other. Come down and we will believe." But He did not come down. And why? Because it is practical to come down; because it is *human* to come down; because if He came down He never would have saved us! But it is Divine to be impractical; it is Divine to hang there!

THE FUNDAMENTAL LIBERTY

DELIVERED ON FEBRUARY 2, 1936

THUS FAR we have considered the two conditions of the prodigal's return; namely, entering into himself or recognizing the primacy of the spiritual, and secondly, admitting a sense of need for the Bread of the Father's House. We now come to the third condition: the recognition of Authority. In the words of our Lord, the prodigal then said: "I will arise, and will go to my father."

These words of the prodigal revealed two astounding admissions born of the ashes of a sad and disillusioned life. The first was that there is no escaping authority. The prodigal saw now that the choice before him was not whether he would accept or reject the authority of his father, but whether he would accept the authority of the father or the authority of his passions and his vicious habits. Secondly, the prodigal had finally to admit that the authority of the Father's House which he once thought so enslaving was the only authority which could ever make him free.

Now, to apply this to Western Civilization. It, too, like the prodigal, is finding out to its own chagrin that in

THE PRODIGAL WORLD

rejecting the authority of the Father's House, it did not escape authority, but it only substituted one authority for another, and an authority of a tyrannical kind, like the passions of the prodigal. Following the example of the prodigal, our civilization threw off all authority: First the authority of the Church, then the authority of the Bible, and finally the authority of religion and morals in the political, economic, and social order. This break with authority created a false sense of liberty such as the prodigal felt in the first wild moments of dissipation. Liberty was bound to be distorted once it was torn away from Truth and Divine Responsibility. Freedom became synonymous with doing whatever you pleased, whether it was good or evil, or believing whatever you pleased whether it was true or false. The result was that freedom degenerated into a form of "selfishness," expressed itself in such slogans as "be yourself," frowned upon all forms of restraint and sacrifice as contrary to the individual libido, and ended in what might be called the exaltation and glorification of the ego.

But the modern man soon discovered that he is the slave of that which overcomes him, and that he really had not escaped authority. He had only substituted one kind of authority for another—in rejecting the authority of God, he became subject to the authority of Caesar. This came about because our civilization having lost the religious sanctions of authority, sought some obligatory organization as the

FULTON J. SHEEN

sole means of escaping absolute chaos and degeneration. Like camels who run together when frightened, so these prophets of false liberty, when lightened by the collapse of every ideal they believed to be true, sought refuge in the human collective, in the mass, or in the State. It was a way of trying to get collective control over that which should have been controlled by a social religion informing the individual conscience. The abuses resulting from a liberty which was only selfishness reached such enormous proportions that political authority had to step in and re-establish itself over economic forces which had long escaped from it and were now mocking it. That is why the reaction against false liberty tended to dictatorship. In some nations it did not stop with the State attempting to enforce the legally just as a substitute for the morally righteous! It reached a point where the State assumed complete control over the temporal and spiritual life of man. A social conscience took the place of a personal conscience. Dictatorship overflowed into the spiritual order; organization became an obsession; social planning became a mania. A unity of ideas and beliefs was imposed upon the submerged personalities by the State, which felt the need of creating an economic unity to replace the spiritual unity whose basis is Christ.

The general effect of the reaction was the substitution of the authority of Caesar for the authority of God; or the mobilization of individual egotists into a collective

THE PRODIGAL WORLD

selfishness, which is Communism. We are witnessing therefore the queer spectacle of a world that began by hating authority, now falling down before an authority more absolute than history has seen since the advent of Christianity. The authority of the Father's House was rejected because it was said to stand in the way of liberty; and now the Prodigal World finds itself the slave of those forces it once thought would make it free. It would not have God with His law of love, now it must have Caesar with his iron law; it would not be subject to the Father, now it must be subject to the citizen of the foreign country.

There is no escaping authority; the prodigal found that out, and the modern world is now finding it out again. Its three hundred year old experiment with liberty has taught it that liberty does not mean the right to violate either the laws of God or man. It wanted an order in which every man was free, and found out too late that in such an order only the strong are free; it wanted a religion in which each man could think out his own beliefs and found it just as absurd as thinking out his own astronomy. Hence the problem is not whether we shall or shall not accept authority; the problem is *which* authority will we accept, the authority of Christ, or the authority of anti-Christ. Our age is now answering that question.

This brings us to the second admission of the prodigal, namely, that the authority of the father which he rejected as

FULTON J. SHEEN

the obstacle to freedom was the only authority which could ever make him free. Our civilization too must eventually come to realize that the Church which for the last three hundred years has been attacked as the enemy of liberty and freedom now stands alone as the bulwark and guarantee of liberty, and that every word she utters is a protest against the new slavery of the modern man.

The new slavery is different from the old. The old slavery was physical. A man under that regime was not permitted either the fruits of the labor of his hands or the rewards of the sweat of his brow; his work, his talents, his body, his wife and his children, belonged to the man who owned him. The new slavery is not physical but spiritual and moral. It affects sometimes the body as in Russia, but principally it affects the soul, the conscience, the will, and the personality of man; it takes its roots into the more human and divine part of him, asserts the primacy of the economic order over the human, and subjects him to the race, the class, the Proletariat, the State which owns him and whose dominant passion is the Passion for Power.

Against this new slavery whose venom strikes deeper roots than the old, the Church has risen in protest. Why has she condemned Birth Control, Sterilization? Why has she anathematized Communism? Why has she condemned employers who would deny workmen the right to organize? Why has she frowned upon workmen who

THE PRODIGAL WORLD

would abolish all private property? Simply because each of these things is a violation of the Rights of Man; because a human personality has certain inalienable rights which no one can take away from him; in a word, because a man is to be measured and judged not by what he produces for the State but by what he is destined to be by God.

This is a new role for the Church. Yes, she has had to defend liberties before, but they were liberties of the supernatural order. Up until the close of the nineteenth century she had to assert the freedom of man to accept grace, against Calvinistic Determinism; but now she is called upon, not to defend liberty in the order of grace, but liberty in the order of nature. Before she had to go forth to battle for the freedom of a man to be a saint; now she has to fight for the freedom of a man to be a man. This is a sad state of affairs when Christ in His Mystical Body has to remind the world of those truths which even the pagans believed, namely, the right of a man to be free, to be captain of his own fate and destiny, and the right to pray, "Our Father, Who art in heaven," instead of "Soviet Union which art in Russia."

If the world continues to get so far away from fundamentals, a day may yet come when the Church will go out to battle in defense of the truth that two and two make four, that grass is green in summer, and that snow is white. Her excommunications of the future will not be against those

FULTON J. SHEEN

who deny that there are three persons in one God, but against those who deny that every citizen in a State is a person. She has been the defender of the revealed liberties of the world; now, she is to be the defender of the last liberty of all, the freedom of man.

Rob man of the freedom of serving and loving God and you have robbed him of his manhood. Men with minds that can fly cannot be kept in cages; men with divine home-sickness cannot find homes under roofs; men destined to be filled with Life and Truth and Love cannot be satisfied with only their bellies filled. Rob them of their God, which is the root of all the liberties of man, and they will build a false god as they are doing now. When Moses was absent for forty days on the mountain-top communing with the Living God, the children of Israel made for themselves a golden calf. And today when the people in Russia and Germany and Mexico are deprived of God, they make the iron calf of the State and the Race; if they are not permitted to walk in processions to the Mother of God, they will dance about tractors; if they are forbidden to adore God in a tabernacle they will bow down before an embalmed corpse and a paraffined cheek in the Kremlin of the Red Square. That is why the religion of Russia is the opium of the People—it does not deny God who was the root of all their liberties; it falsifies His image and makes them slaves. But this will not satisfy them long. Communism may build

THE PRODIGAL WORLD

Babels, a thousand factories, schools and hospitals, but their Babels will crumble without the Cornerstone; the products of their factories will be without excellence, the dying in their hospitals will not be healed, the scholars in their schools will not learn wisdom because they have forgotten that a cow is satisfied when its stomach is full, but not a man. He is not satisfied until he is free, and he is not free until he can love when he pleases, and he cannot love when he pleases until he loves the One for Whom he was made—the God whose name is Love!

THE SENSE OF SIN

DELIVERED ON FEBRUARY 9, 1936

THE FINAL CONDITION of the return to the Father's House was a recognition, on the part of the prodigal, of the sense of sin. This condition is revealed by the following words of the parable: "I will arise and will go to my father, and will say to him: I have sinned against heaven and before thee; I am not worthy to be called thy son; make me as one of thy hired servants." Herein is combined the double element of true redemption: an admission of sin; "I have sinned," and the need of penance, "make me as one of thy hired servants."

Our Blessed Lord never once hints in the parable, when the young man returned with a face furrowed with the hard lines of sin, that he ever offered any excuse for his sinfulness. There is no record, there is not even a hint, that he attempted to excuse himself or to extenuate his prodigality. He offered no theory about sin; he did not say it was a fall in the evolutionary process; he did not blame his environment or his wicked companions; he did not tell his father that he had inherited a queer Freudian complex from him;

THE PRODIGAL WORLD

he did not say that moral decline is only a myth and that sin is just an illusion; he asked no Lippmann to write a Preface to Morals saying men could no longer live according to traditional morality, and must therefore have a new moral to suit unmoral ways of living. He did not excuse himself by saying that a man was justified in sowing his wild oats and then forgetting, living for the present and having no responsibility for the past. There was none of these things in the mouth of the prodigal, and much less was there any such thought in his heart. Out of its torn and bleeding self there came only tear-drippings, a deep recognition of the horror of sin and the need of pardon and redemption. "I have sinned against heaven and before thee."

But sin is the one thing modern civilization will not admit. Instead it believes itself incapable of sinning, and places the blame not in man who violates the moral law, but in the moral law which it says is behind the times. The result is, we are living in a time when old forms of sensationalism of a generation ago are now regarded as banal; when words such as "obedience" and "purity" which once stood for the sacred, now, in our era of carnality, stand either for weakness or restraint of liberty. If there is any way of describing our civilization it is to say we are at the penumbra, i.e., at that point where light fades and shadows begin. We have not yet crossed the line, because whether the world admits it or not, it is still living on the spiritual

FULTON J. SHEEN

capital which the Church divided unto it four centuries ago. Everything that is good, everything that is charitable, everything that is noble in our civilization, is a reflection of abiding Christian principles and a splinter from the Cross of Christ. But the vision of the Cross is fading; the borderland between light and darkness is growing dimmer and the world is about to pass over into the hinterland of darkness and ruin.

The Church has felt this moral decline. She notes the complete absence of rational objections against her. Never before has she been so impoverished for good strong intellectual opposition as at the present time. There are no foemen worthy of her steel. The opposition today is not intellectual, but moral. Men are no longer objecting to the Church because of the way they think, but because of the way they live. They no longer have difficulty with her Creed, but with her commandments. They remain outside her saving waters, not because they cannot accept the doctrine of Three Persons in One God but because they cannot accept the moral of two persons in one flesh; not because Infallibility is too complex, but because avoidance of Birth Control is too hard; not because the Eucharist is too sublime, but because Penance is too exacting. Briefly, the heresy of our day is not the heresy of thought—it is the heresy of action.

Our whole civilization is pervaded by a general atrophy

THE PRODIGAL WORLD

of the vital conviction that there is a righteous purpose sovereign in history. Men today model their lives solely in relation to economic interests rather than the common good and the glory of God. What adds to the seriousness of it is that the world's fallen state is accompanied, not by an increased, but by a decreased sense of sin. It is sinning more, but is less mindful of its gravity. It offends God more, but it is worried less about its offense. How rarely do we find anyone outside of the Father's House doing penance for his sins? How often does a writer of immoral books, when he comes to the consciousness of the souls be has polluted, end his days in prayer and sacrifice? How often do we hear of an industrialist coming forward and saying: "My violation of the virtue of Justice is the cause of the depression and I must make amends for my sins before God?" Rarely indeed is it recorded of a modern sinner, that he seeks to enter the Kingdom of God by doing penance. And why? Because the modern ideal is not goodness, but success. Such an ideal makes penance impossible. Paganism sinned too, but the sin of modern paganism has the added seriousness of having betrayed an ideal which the older pagans had not—namely the ideal of Christ.

By this I do not mean to say that when the world accepted the faith and morals of the Church that the world was free of sinners. As a matter of fact there were men just as wicked in the 13th century as there are in the twentieth;

FULTON J. SHEEN

there were Christians just as immoral in the age of martyrs as there are today—though there were not so many. But there is this great difference between the sinners of a Christianized civilization and the sinners of our day—the sinners of the Christian civilization *knew they were sinners*; the sinners of modern civilization think they are saints. The sinners of the Christian civilization broke the law, but admitted the law was right; the sinners of modern civilization break the law and say that the law is wrong. The sinners of Christian ages knew they were wrong, but they wished to be right. The sinners of our day on the contrary do wrong, and do not want to be right. There is hope for any civilization which breaks a law but never calls into question the truth of the law; but there is no hope for a civilization that breaks a law and then *denies it*. Man is powerless to resist evil if he does not recognize it as such, just as he is hopeless if he is wounded and does not wish to be healed.

It may take a long time before the modern world is willing to cry out with the prodigal: "I have sinned"; but until that day arrives it can expect no healing ointment for its broken wings. There is no redemption except from sin; there is no hope for betterment until there has been an admission of failure. Our social structure must one day admit the fallacy of "business is business"; it must judge its economic policies, not by their feasibility, but by their morality; and it must confess that economics and politics

THE PRODIGAL WORLD

are but branches of moral theology and philosophy, i.e., that they can be sinful if they are in violation of the ultimate end of man. It must admit that the moral necessity of attaining the full perfection of man's personality circumscribes human action in the domestic, political, economic, and religious spheres; that every act is a moral act, even a religious act; that nothing is excluded, whether it be the selling of a can of milk or of a great corporation. Hence economic policy can save a man's soul as well as damn it. Morality is involved in the realities of industry, finance, and government, and the assumption that these things are governed by non-ethical forces is false. Business can crucify Christ just as well as Pride, and therefore it has just as much need of Redemption.

And what is to be done about it? Well, what would we do if we found a live whale on top of the Alps—that is, if we wanted to save it? We would try to restore it as quickly as possible to its environment. And that is the only thing to be done with the world. Put it back in its environment of religion and morality. And all the discussion about politics and economics divorced from the moral order is just as stupid as to legislate for whales on mountain tops. It is a change of heart, of mind, of soul, and not a new economics which is needed, and this new heart can be found only at the foot of the Cross where things are measured according to their true worth. Once men see that Cross elevated before their eyes at the elevation of the Host, they begin to see that three score and ten years of life is a time for testing—a moment taken out of eternal life in which to say "yea" or "nay" to Divine Love.

Once the world is restored to the environment of Calvary it will see that it need not step down to ruin and despair, for the important thing about sin is not its sinfulness, but the fact that it can be redeemed. Once the Cross is set up again before the eyes of men and placarded at the cross-roads of civilization, as it was centuries ago, men will realize that redemption is social, and that we are our brothers' keepers, in helping one another to a fresh start even though it is a late start. Economics can still provide men with the *means* of existence, but only the Cross can offer the *object* of existence, which determines the morality of the means.

But take away the vision of that Cross which leads to the crown beyond the grave, and what answer can we make to the poor who would steal from the rich out of envy, and the rich who would crush the poor out of lust? Take away the Cross and what hope shall we give the sinner who wishes to be clean, the sick who have borne their pain with patience, the just who have suffered unjustly? Take away the Cross which stands suspended between heaven and earth and you take away the bridge by which God descends to man and man ascends to God.

THE PRODIGAL WORLD

The Cross will not relieve the world of suffering, for its kingdom of happiness is not here; it has not saved modern civilization, because modern civilization has not tried it, but only its substitutes and imitations. However, it does secure a recognition of a supernatural criterion and a normal pattern of life, which, if accepted, would enable "the mass of men to fulfill their destiny on earth without being obliged to heroism"; it does provide an eternal end rather than a temporal end as the basis of social action, and that means everything; it does make life reasonable by assuring man that he lives in a world of good and evil opportunity, where his choice must be a matter of significance for himself and his fellowmen; it does influence the economic order by denouncing the immorality of slave wages for working-men in industry, of calling men "superfluous" in a universe where every man has an immortal soul, and of suppressing man for the sake of the State when a man is a citizen of the Kingdom of God as well as the Kingdom of Caesar.

In comparison to it, all subsequent revolutions are but trivial upstarts, for they failed to affect the soul of society; even the Communistic revolution was incomplete for it still leaves hate, and does not say, "Forgive"; it still leaves earthliness and does not say: "This day thou shalt be with me in paradise"; it still leaves despair, and does not say: "Father, into thy hands I commend my spirit." Communism is not revolutionary enough—it still leaves man where he falls.

FULTON J. SHEEN

Be not fooled by those who would save us without the Cross. There is no escaping the Cross, for the simple reason that there is no goal gained without the effort and no victory won without the battle. To keep whispering to ourselves sweet but false consolations, to look for the end when we are only at the beginning, to go round the Cross instead of taking it up, these are but the materials out of which a cross is made—and a cross where one bar is at variance and contradiction with another, the most insoluble mystery of all.

But to enter into that higher plane of making earth a stepping stone to heaven, where nobility stands the test, where love spells sacrifice, where the horizontal bar of death meets the vertical bar of life in the Person of Christ on the Cross reconciling both—this is the Crucifix, wherein we confess not the mysterious ways of Job, but enter into them for our eternal joy and consolation. Once united with the Crucified as we are in the Mass, then we begin to understand that everywhere else others promise us sin excused, sin discounted, sin denied, sin explained away, but only at the foot of the Cross do we ever experience the beautiful divine contradiction of *sin forgiven*.

THE RETURN FROM EXILE

DELIVERED ON FEBRUARY 16, 1936

THE CONCLUSION of the parable of the prodigal son pictures the father meeting the prodigal. The father met the prodigal on the road, according to the Scriptures, when he was "yet a great way off." These words have a meaning for us in the modern parallel of the story which we are considering in this course of radio lectures. They imply two things: On the part of the prodigal a recognition that the Father's House, or the Church, is the only place the prodigal children of Western Civilization can find the Freedom and the Peace they crave; on the part of the Father's House, or the Church, a recognition of the necessity of hopefulness, and the need of going out into the roads and thoroughfares of the world to meet the prodigal children in an embrace of love, the ring of fidelity, and the cloak of charity.

Firstly, the prodigal children must return to the Father's House not only and uniquely because it will make them prosperous, but because it will give them Peace and Freedom, which are the conditions of temporal prosperity. The prodigal son did not return because he wanted the banquet

FULTON J. SHEEN

of the fatted calf. He returned because he wanted the love, the forgiveness, and the authority of the father's house. The fatted calf was the by-product of his return: not the goal that was sought. In like manner Western Civilization must seek first the Kingdom of God and His Justice, and all these other things will be added unto it. The fatted calf of earthly prosperity is only secondary: it may or may not follow. What is important is the right relation of lives to God. This was the characteristic note of the teaching of our Lord and therefore of His Church; namely, what might be called *political and economic relativity*, namely, social amelioration as a *by-product* of Christianity. Systems of politics and economics are of secondary importance, but not primary; not absolute, but relative. Civilization can be great under a monarchy or a parliament, under a democracy or under imperialism; civilization can be good under free trade or tariff, gold standards or silver standards; but no civilization can be good unless it serves and loves God. Hence to Satan who would have given Him all the political and economic kingdoms of earth our Lord flung one word "begone"; to those who would trap Him into a dispute about conquered and conquering peoples he said: "Render therefore to Caesar the things that are Caesar's; and to God, the things that are God's"; and to those who would make Him intervene in matters of money He asks: "who hath appointed me judge, or divider, over you?"

THE PRODIGAL WORLD

In like manner, Western civilization must not measure the value of Christ's Church in terms of the fatted calf, increased profits, and favorable balance of trade.

The same false notion about the Church producing prosperity prevailed in Rome at the time of its decline. Alaric came to Rome about the beginning of the fifth century, forced open the Salarian gate and sacked the Capitol. The whole world was stirred by the fall of this mighty Cedar of Libanus. Not since the invasion of Rome by the Gauls eight hundred years before had the capitol been so threatened, invaded, and outraged. Rome felt she was invulnerable because eternal, little realizing that she was eternal not because of the force of her arms, but because a fisherman came to dwell there. Immediately the cry went up: "We have perished because we have become Christians. Christianity has failed us! We are not as powerful, we are not as mighty, we are not as great as we were with the old gods Aeneas brought from Troy. We are weak with the weakness of the God on a Cross Peter brought back from Calvary. Christianity has brought us bad luck!"

St. Augustine in far-off Africa heard the cry and answered its challenge in his mighty work "The City of God." He reminded the fallen empire that it had fallen, not because it was Christian, but because it had failed to be Christian. He admitted Rome had done great things for the world; that it had been prosperous and had given man

FULTON J. SHEEN

a common law and a common language. Yet these benefits had been purchased by war, slavery, and oppression of the weak, and in the end served only senseless luxury and the mobs of the amphitheater. He told them in no uncertain terms that Christianity, although possessing a social philosophy and character, never promised to be a social panacea for all the ills of humankind; that the world was only a road and not a house to live in, that life is a pilgrimage to another city, and not the art of making a heaven on earth, that the benefits of Christianity are not restricted to the material. Rather they are like the blood of Christ which regenerates us unto life everlasting.

The world would not listen to Augustine. The world then believed as it believes now, that civilization is identical with prosperity, and that Christianity fails when it fails to make the world prosperous. Within the Church as well as outside, Augustine was begged to be quiet about Christianity bringing supernatural benefits. Everywhere men pleaded: "Si taceat de Roma." "If he would only shut up about Rome." But he did not shut up. He preached and cried down the error that the sole business of Christianity is business. And in this day and age when the Father of Christendom reminds the world that its economics and politics can not be divorced from Christian standards of morality, that its social structure can not be made right until men make their peace with God, and that society can

THE PRODIGAL WORLD

not be improved except by reforming the individuals who make it up, the cry of Augustine's day is hurled in his face: O si taceat de Roma! Oh if he would only shut up about Rome, about the Sanctity of Marriage, about Education built upon Christ, about Grace, about the Sacraments and Eternal Life. But in these days as in the days of Augustine there must be no silence. Spiritual regeneration must condition social reconstruction. There is no other way than the way of the Lord. He, the living Bread, came on earth when there was a famine and was born in a little city called Bethlehem, the House of Bread. He came on earth when crimes were great and powerful and said that he who took the sword would perish by the sword; He came at a time when slaves were ill treated and yet preached, "servants, obey your master"; He came on earth when men would have proclaimed Him King of their economics and politics and said: "My kingdom is not of this world"; He came on earth to a people who hated Caesar, and paid tribute to Caesar; He came on earth when men judged Him by His earthly power and said: "Take up your cross and follow Me."

This is the doctrine the Church is preaching today. No other truth than the spiritual can save our civilization. Talking about the Stars and Stripes will not save a country that has been blessed abundantly by God and then forgets God. There are other stars and other stripes than those in our flag and they are the only ones that will ever save

FULTON J. SHEEN

us—the stars and stripes of Christ, by whose stars we are illumined and by whose stripes we are healed.

On the other hand, the Father's House has its obligation to prodigal Western civilization, and that is to go out on the road even though it is yet a long way off, and make the return easy. The Father's House is inoperative except by and through those who are in it.

The Church is the Mystical Body of Christ. Each Catholic therefore is Christ in his little world. Our Lord has no other feet with which to go about doing good than ours; He has no other cheeks to turn to those who preach class warfare than our own; He has no other lips to teach those who sit in the superstition of the Gentiles than our own. Christ fails in the measure we fail to be Christ-like. No one is unimportant; no action is a-moral or a-Catholic; every thought and every deed has spiritual significance. Out to the roads therefore to meet the prodigal! Never before in four hundred years has the world been so willing to return; seldom since the Incarnation have the average man and woman, oppressed with a sense of false values and ambiguous standards, been so disposed, as they are today, to receive spiritual guidance. And the way they are to be infused is through Catholic Action, or the working of the Pentecostal spirit through every influential cell of the Mystical Body. One thing however we must recognize is that the influence which will make for the civilization of the

THE PRODIGAL WORLD

future will come not from above but from *below*. During the last century, when Liberalism flourished, practically all the influences of social life came from *above*; that is, from the university, the modern prophet, the high-tone, literary magazines, retired business men turned philanthropists, and in general, from the comfortable strata of society. But the influences which are moulding society today are from *below*, from the proletariat, the working man, the father without a job, the hungry women and children, the people whose wants are too many and whose rights are too few, the great mass who follow bad leaders because they have no good ones, the socially disinherited and the economically dispossessed. The leadership today has shifted to the *masses*; the makers of the world today are not the men who lead and inspire the masses; they are the men who reflect the masses; the collectivity creates them, but they do not create it.

The proletariat then has an historical mission for the future; the disinherited laborers have a messianic role for generations yet unborn. The proletarian, and not the university professor, is the raw material of future civilization. The question then is: Who will possess the proletariat first, Christ or anti-Christ? The Church or Communism? If the Truth does not get to them, error will. The duty of Catholics at the present time is to go down to the disinherited group and form a Catholic proletarian culture, just as vigorous and just as zealous as any Communist proletariat. The common man may not be socially proper, he may not have a college education, he may not know how to act in our drawing rooms, but he holds the future in his hands. Both the Church and civilization will draw their strength from such a man. Hence down to the masses, or in the words of Frederick Ozanam: *Passons aux barbares*. Pass on to the proletariat; shift them from the circumference to the center, from emptiness to a vision of spiritual realities. Pass on to the masses, teach them not to spend all their energies in finding solutions for transitory problems, but to lay the foundations of a new order. If they are rebellious against law and order, justice and morality, country, and God, it is a reminder of our own unfulfilled duty. They are not altogether to blame if they hate the Church; we would hate it too, if we believed the same lies about it that they do. But whatever be their mentality, they are the raw material of the future; they are the stuff which will compose the Mystical Body of the next generation. It was from the same type of man the Church in the first few centuries recruited her martyrs. Because they are Communists, they are not to be despised; because they are pagans, they are not to be hated. The Church has no fear of paganism. We were born in paganism; we saw it die, and by the grace of God, we will see it die again. The first time we killed it was during a persecution. And that is when we shall kill it again! The Catacombs may once more house martyrs!

CALVARY AND SACRIFICE

DELIVERED ON FEBRUARY 23, 1936

THERE ARE CERTAIN THINGS in life which are too beautiful to be forgotten, such as the love of one's mother. Hence we treasure her picture. The love of soldiers who sacrificed themselves for their country is likewise too beautiful to be forgotten, hence we revere that memory on Memorial Day. But the greatest blessing which ever came to this earth was the visitation of the Son of God in the form and habit of man. That Life is above all lives too beautiful to be forgotten, hence we treasure the Divinity of His *Words* in Sacred Scripture, and the Charity of His *Deeds* in our daily actions. Unfortunately this is all some souls remember, namely His Words and His Deeds; important as these are, they are not the greatest characteristic of the Divine Savior. The most sublime act in the history of Christ was His *Death*. Death is always important for it seals a destiny. Any dying man is a scene. Any dying scene is a sacred place. That is why the great literature of the past which has touched on the emotions surrounding death has never passed out of date. But of all deaths in the record of man,

FULTON J. SHEEN

none was more important than the Death of Christ. Everyone else who was ever born into the world, came into it to *live*: our Lord came into it to *die*. Death was a stumbling block to the life of Socrates, but it was the crown to the life of Christ. He Himself told us that He came "to give his life a redemption for many"; that no one could take away His life; that He would lay it down of Himself.

If then Death was the supreme moment for which Christ lived it was therefore the *one thing* He wished to have remembered above all others. He did not ask that men should write down His words into a Scripture; He did not ask that His kindness to the poor, the lame, and the blind should be recorded in history; but He did ask that men remember His Death. And in order that its memory might not be any haphazard narrative on the part of men, He Himself instituted the precise way it should be recalled. Man has instituted Memorial Day to recall the death of soldiers in the field of battle, but Christ instituted His own Memorial to re-enact His Death on the gibbet of the Cross.

The memorial was instituted the night before He died, at what has since been called "The Last Supper." Taking bread into His hands, He said: "This is my body, which shall be delivered for you," i.e., delivered unto death. Then over the chalice of wine He said, "This is my blood of the new testament, which shall be shed for many unto remission of sins." Thus in an unbloody symbolic manner of the parting

THE PRODIGAL WORLD

of the Blood from the Body, did Christ pledge Himself to death in the sight of God and men and represent His death which was to come the next afternoon at three.† He was offering Himself as a Victim to be immolated, and that men might never forget that "greater love than this no man hath, that a man lay down his life for his friends," He gave the Divine Command: "Do this for a commemoration of me."

The following day what He had prefigured and foreshadowed He realized in its completeness, as He was crucified between two thieves and His Blood drained from His Body for the redemption of the world.

The Church which Christ founded has not only preserved the words He spoke, and the wonders He wrought; it has also taken Him seriously when He said: "Do this for a commemoration of me." And that action whereby we re-enact His Death on the Cross is the Sacrifice of the

---

† "Death is put before us in a symbol, by means of that sacramental parting of the Blood from the Body; but death at the same time already pledged to God for all its worth, as well as all its awful reality, by the expressive language of the Sacred Symbol. The price of our sins shall be paid down on Calvary; but here the liability is incurred by our Redeemer, and subscribed in His very Blood" (Maurice de la Taille, S.J., *Catholic Faith in the Holy Eucharist*, p. 115). "There were not two distinct and complete sacrifices offered by Christ, one in the Cenacle, the other on Calvary. There was a sacrifice at the Last Supper, but it was the sacrifice of Redemption; and there was a sacrifice on the Cross, but it was the self-same sacrifice continued and completed. The Supper and the Cross made up one complete sacrifice" (Maurice de la Taille, S.J., *The Mystery of Faith and Human Opinion*, p. 232).

FULTON J. SHEEN

Mass, in which we do as a memorial what He did at the Last Supper as the prefiguration of His Passion.†

Hence the Mass is to us the crowning act of Christian worship. A pulpit in which the words of our Lord are repeated does not unite us to Him; a choir in which sweet sentiments are sung brings us no closer to His Cross than to His Ascension. A temple without an altar of sacrifice is non-existent among primitive peoples, and is meaningless among Christians. And so in the Catholic Church the altar and not the pulpit or the choir is the center of worship, for there is re-enacted the Memorial of His Passion. Its value does not depend on him who says it, or on him who hears it; it depends on Him Who is the One High Priest and Victim, Jesus Christ our Lord. With Him we are united, in spite of our nothingness; in a certain sense, we lose our individuality for the time being; we unite our intellect and

---

† "He offered the Victim to be immolated; we offer it as immolated of old. We offer the eternal Victim of the Cross, once made and forever enduring... The Mass is a sacrifice because it is our oblation of the Victim once immolated, even as the Supper was the oblation of the Victim to be immolated" (De la Taille, *The Mystery of Faith and Human Opinion*, pp. 239-240). The Mass is not only a commemoration, it is a living representation of the sacrifice of the cross. "In this Divine Sacrifice which takes place at the Mass is contained and immolated in an unbloody manner, the same Christ that was offered once for all in blood upon the Cross...It is one and the same Victim, one and the same High Priest, Who made the offering through the ministry of His priests today, after having offered Himself upon the cross yesterday; only the manner of the oblation is different" (Council of Trent. Sess. 22).

our will, our heart and our soul, our body and our blood, so intimately with Christ, that the Heavenly Father sees not so much *us* with our imperfection, but rather sees us *in Him*, the Beloved Son in whom He is well pleased. The Mass is for that reason the greatest event in the history of mankind; the only Holy Act which keeps the wrath of God from a sinful world, because it holds the Cross between, and renews that decisive moment when our sad and tragic humanity journeyed suddenly forth to the fullness of supernatural life.

What is important at this point is that we take the proper mental attitude toward the Mass, and remember this important fact, that the Sacrifice of the Cross is not something which happened nineteen hundred years ago. It is still happening. It is not something past like the signing of the Declaration of Independence; it is an abiding drama on which the curtain has not yet rung down. Let it not be believed that it happened a long time ago, and therefore no more concerns us than anything else in the past. Calvary belongs to all times and to all places. That is why, when our Blessed Lord ascended the heights of Calvary, He was fittingly stripped of His garments: He would save the world without the trappings of the world. Adam lost his innocence and hence sought to clothe himself to hide the foulness of the temple of his body. Our Lord kept His innocence, hence He had no need of clothing that covers shame.

FULTON J. SHEEN

His garments belonged to time, for they localized Him, and fixed Him as a dweller in Galilee. Now that He was shorn of them to be utterly dispossessed of earthly things, He belonged not to Galilee, not to a Roman province, but to the world. He became the universal poor man of the world. Henceforth He would belong to no one people, but to all men.

To express further the universality of the Redemption, the cross was erected at the crossroads of civilization, at a central point between the three great cultures of Jerusalem, Rome, and Athens, in whose names He was crucified. This fact was placarded before the eyes of men, to arrest the careless, to appeal to the thoughtless, to arouse the worldly. It was the one inescapable fact the cultures and civilizations of His day could not resist. It is also the one inescapable fact of our day which we cannot resist.

The figures at the Cross were symbols of all who crucify. We were there in our representatives. What we are doing now to the Mystical Christ, they were doing in our names to the Historical Christ. If we are envious of the good, for example—for goodness is a reproach to the evil—we were there in the Scribes and Pharisees. If we are fearful of losing some temporal advantage by embracing Divine Truth and Love, we were there in Pilate. If we trust in material forces and seek to conquer through the world instead of through the spirit, we were there in Herod. And so the story goes on

THE PRODIGAL WORLD

for the typical sins of the world. They all blind us to the fact that He is God. There was therefore a kind of inevitability about the Crucifixion. Men who were free to sin, were also free to crucify.

As long as there is sin in the world the Crucifixion is a reality. As the poet has put it:

> I saw the son of man go by
> Crowned with a crown of thorns.
> Was it not finished Lord, said I,
> And all the anguish borne?
>
> He turned on me His awful eyes;
> Hast thou not understood?
> So every soul is a Calvary
> And every sin a rood.

We were there during that Crucifixion. The drama was already completed as far as the Vision of Christ was concerned, but it had not yet been unfolded to all men and all places and all times. If a motion picture reel, for example, were conscious of itself, it would know the drama from beginning to end, but the spectators in the theater would not know it until they had seen it unrolled upon the screen. In like manner, our Lord on the Cross saw in His Eternal Mind, the whole drama of history, the story of each individual soul, and how later on it would react to His Crucifixion; but though He saw all, we could not know how we would react to the Cross until we were unrolled upon the screen of time. We were not conscious of being present there on Calvary that day, but He was conscious of our presence. Today we know the role we played in the theatre of Calvary, by the way we live and act now in the theatre of the twentieth century.

That is why Calvary is actual, why the Cross is the crisis, why in a certain sense the scars are still open, why pain still stands deified, and why blood like falling stars is still dropping upon our souls. There is no escape from the fact, not even by denying it as the Pharisees did, not even by selling Christ as Judas did, not even by crucifying Him as the executioners did, for the Cross is still set up in the world.

But how is it visible? Where shall we find Calvary perpetuated? We shall find Calvary renewed, re-enacted, represented, as we have seen, in the Mass. Calvary is one with the Mass, and the Mass is one with Calvary, for in both there is the same Priest and Victim. The Seven Last Words are like the seven parts of the Mass. And just as there are seven notes in music admitting an infinite variety of harmonies and combinations, so too on the Cross there are seven divine notes, which the dying Christ has sent down the centuries, all of which combine in the beautiful harmony of the Drama of the World's Redemption.

THE PRODIGAL WORLD

Picture then the High Priest Christ leaving the sacristy of heaven for the altar of Calvary. He has already put on the vestment of our human nature, the maniple of our suffering, the stole of priesthood, the chasuble of the Cross. Calvary is His Cathedral; the rock of Calvary is the altar stone; the sun turning to red is the sanctuary lamp; Mary and John are the living side altars; the host is His Body; the wine is His Blood. He is upright as Priest, yet He is prostrate as Victim. Christ is going to His altar. We shall assist at His First Mass.

THE FIRST WORD

DELIVERED ON MARCH 1, 1936

"Father, forgive them, for they know not what they do."
(LUKE 23:34)

THE MASS begins with the Confiteor. The Confiteor is a prayer in which we confess our sins and ask the Blessed Mother and the Saints to intercede to God for our forgiveness, for only the clean of heart can see God. Our Blessed Lord too begins His Mass with the Confiteor. But His Confiteor differs from ours in this. He has no sins to confess. He is God and therefore sinless. "Which of you shall convince me of sin?" His Confiteor then can not be a prayer for the forgiveness of *His* sins; but it can be a prayer for the forgiveness of *our* sins.

Others would have screamed, cursed, writhed, as the nails pierced their hands and feet. But no vindictiveness finds place in the Savior's breast; no appeal comes from His lips for vengeance on His murderers; He breathes no prayer for strength to bear His pain. Incarnate Love forgets injury, forgets pain, and in that moment of concentrated agony

THE PRODIGAL WORLD

reveals something of the height, the depth, and the breadth of the wonderful love of God, as He says His Confiteor: "Father, forgive them, for they know not what they do."

He did not say "Forgive me," but "Forgive them." The moment of death was certainly the one most likely to produce confession of sin, for conscience in the last solemn hours does assert its authority; and yet not a single sigh of penitence escaped His lips. He was associated with sinners, but never associated with sin. In death as well as life, He was unconscious of a single unfulfilled duty to His Heavenly Father. And why? Because a sinless man is not just a man; He is more than mere man. He is sinless, because He is God—and there is the difference. We draw our prayers from the depths of our consciousness of sin: He drew His silence from His own intrinsic sinlessness. That one word "Forgive" proves Him to be the Son of God.

Notice the grounds on which He asked His Heavenly Father to forgive us—"Because they know not what they do." When anyone injures us, or blames us wrongly, we say: "They should have known better." But when we sin against God, He finds a reason for forgiveness—our ignorance.

There is no redemption for the fallen angels. The blood drops that fell from the cross on Good Friday in that Mass of Christ, did not touch the spirits of the fallen angels. Why? Because they knew what they were doing! They saw all the consequences of their acts, just as clearly as we see that two and two make four, or that a thing cannot exist and exist at the same time. Truths of this kind when understood cannot be taken back; they are irrevocable and eternal. Hence when they decided to rebel against Almighty God, there was no taking back the decision. They *knew* what they were doing!

But with us it is different. We do not see the consequences of our acts as clearly as the angels; we are of weaker stuff; we are ignorant. But if we did know that every sin of pride wove a crown of thorns for the Head of Christ; if we knew that every contradiction of His Divine command made for Him the sign of contradiction, the Cross; if we knew that every grasping avaricious act nailed His hands, and every journey into the byways of sin dug His feet; if we knew how good God is and still went on sinning, we would never be saved. Why we would be *damned*. It is only our ignorance of the infinite love of the Sacred Heart that brings us within the hearing of His Confiteor from the Cross: "Father, forgive them, for they know not what they do."

These words, let it be deeply graven on our souls, do not constitute an *excuse* for continued sin, but a *motive* for contrition and penance. Forgiveness is not a denial of sin. Our Lord does not *deny* the horrible fact of sin, and that is where the modern world is wrong. It explains sin away: it ascribes it to a fall in the evolutionary process, to

THE PRODIGAL WORLD

a survival of ancient taboos; it identifies it with psychological verbiage. In a word, the modern world *denies* sin. Our Lord reminds us that it is the most terrible of all realities. Otherwise why does it give Sinlessness a cross? Why does it shed innocent blood? Why does it have such awful associations: blindness, compromise, cowardice, hatred, and cruelty? Why does it now lift itself out of the realm of the impersonal and assert itself as personal by nailing Innocence to a gibbet? An abstraction cannot do that. But sinful man can. Hence He, who loved men unto death, allowed sin to wreak its vengeance upon Him, in order that they might forever understand its horror as the crucifixion of Him who loved them most.

There is no denial of sin here—and yet, with all its horror, the Victim forgives. In that one and the same event, there is the sign of sin's utter depravity and the seal of Divine Forgiveness. From that point on, no man can look upon a Crucifix and say that sin is not serious, nor can he ever say that it cannot be forgiven. By the way He suffered, He revealed the reality of sin; by the way He bore it, He shows His mercy toward the sinner. It is the Victim who has suffered that forgives: and in that combination of a Victim so humanly beautiful, so divinely loving, so wholly innocent, does one find a Great Crime and a Greater Forgiveness. Under the shelter of the Blood of Christ the worst sinners may take their stand; for there is a power in that Blood to turn back the tides of vengeance which threaten to drown the world. The world will give you sin explained away, but only on Calvary do you experience the divine contradiction of sin forgiven. On the Cross Supreme Self-giving and Divine Love transform sin's worst act in the noblest deed and sweetest prayer the world has even seen or heard, the Confiteor of Christ: "Father, forgive them, for they know not what they do."

That word "Forgive," which rang out from the Cross that day when Sin rose to its full strength and then fell defeated by Love, did not die with its echo. A little more than a year before that same Merciful Savior had taken means to prolong forgiveness through space and time, even to the consummation of the world. Gathering the nucleus of His Church round about Him, He said to His Apostles: "Whose sins you shall forgive, they are forgiven." Somewhere in the world today then, the successors of the Apostles have the power to forgive. It is not to the point to ask: But how can man forgive sins?—for man cannot forgive sins. But God can forgive sins *through* man, for is not that the way God forgave His executioners on the cross; namely through the instrumentality of His human nature? Why then is it not reasonable to expect Him still to forgive sins through other human natures to whom He gave that power? And where find those human natures? You know the story of the box which was long ignored and even ridiculed as worthless; and one day it was opened and found to contain the great heart of a giant. In every Catholic Church that box exists. We call it the confessional box. It is ignored and ridiculed by many, but in it is to be found the Sacred Heart of the Forgiving Christ forgiving sinners through the uplifted hand of His priest as He once forgave through His own uplifted hands on the Cross. There is only one forgiveness—the Forgiveness of God. There is only one "Forgive"—the "Forgive" of an Eternal Divine Act in which we come in contact at various moments of time. As the air is always filled with symphony and speech, but we do not hear it unless we tune it in on our radios; so neither do souls feel the joy of that Eternal and Divine "Forgive" unless they are attuned to it in time; and the confessional box is the place where we switch in to that cry from the Cross.

Would to God that our modern mind instead of denying the guilt, would look to the Cross, admit its guilt, and seek forgiveness; would that those who have uneasy consciences that worry them in the light, and haunt them in darkness, would seek relief, not on the plane of medicine but on the plane of Divine Justice; would that they who tell the dark secrets of their minds, would do so not for the sake of sublimation, but for the sake of purgation; would that those poor mortals who shed tears in silence would find an absolving hand to wipe them away. Must it be forever true that the greatest tragedy of life is not what happens to souls, but rather what souls miss—and what greater tragedy is there than to miss the peace of sin forgiven? The Confiteor is at the foot of the altar our cry of unworthiness: the Confiteor from the Cross is our hope of pardon and absolution. The wounds of the Savior were terrible, but the worst wound of all would be to be unmindful that we caused it all. The Confiteor can save us from that, for it is an admission that there is something to be forgiven—and more than we shall ever know.

There is a story told of a nun who was one day dusting a small image of our Blessed Lord in the chapel. In the course of her duty, she let it slip to the floor. She picked it up undamaged, she kissed it, and put it back again in its place, saying, "If you had never fallen, you never would have received that." I wonder if our Blessed Lord does not feel the same way about us, for if we had never sinned, we never could call Him "Savior."

THE SECOND WORD

DELIVERED ON MARCH 8, 1936

*"Amen I say to thee,
this day thou shalt be with me in paradise."*
(LUKE 23:43)

THIS IS NOW the offertory of the Mass, for our Lord is offering Himself to His Heavenly Father. But in order to remind us that He is not offered alone, but in union with us, He unites with His offertory the soul of the thief at the right. To make His ignominy more complete, in a master stroke of malice, they crucified Him between two thieves. He walked among sinners during His life, so now they let Him hang among them at death. But He changed the picture, and made the two thieves the symbols of the sheep and the goats, which will stand at His right and left hand when He comes in the clouds of heaven, with His then triumphant Cross, to judge both the living and the dead.

Both thieves at first reviled and blasphemed, but one of them, whom tradition calls Dismas, turned his head to read the meekness and dignity on the face of the Crucified

FULTON J. SHEEN

Savior. As a piece of coal thrown into the fire is transformed into a bright and glowing thing, so the black soul of this thief thrown into the fires of the Crucifixion glowed with love for the Sacred Heart. While the thief on the left was saying: "If thou be Christ, save thyself and us," the repentant thief rebuked him saying: "Neither dost thou fear God, seeing thou art under the same condemnation. And we indeed justly, for we receive the due reward of our deeds; but this man hath done no evil." That same thief then emitted a plea, not for a place in the seats of the mighty, but only for a remembrance not to be forgotten.

Such sorrow and faith must not go unrewarded. At a moment when the power of Rome could not make Him speak, when His friends thought all was lost and His enemies believed all was won, our Lord broke the silence. He who was the accused, became the Judge; He who was the crucified, became the Divine Assessor of souls, as to the penitent thief He trumpeted the words: "This day thou shalt be with me in paradise." This day—when you said your first prayer and your last; this day—thou shalt be with Me—and where I am, there is Paradise.

With these words our Lord who was offering Himself to His Heavenly Father on the paten of His Cross as the great host, now unites with Him on the paten of the cross the first small host ever offered in the Mass—the host of a repentant thief, a brand plucked from the burning, a sheaf

THE PRODIGAL WORLD

torn from the earthly reapers, the wheat ground in the mill of the crucifixion and made bread for the Eucharist.

Our Lord then does not suffer alone on the Cross: He suffers with us. That is why He united the sacrifice of the thief with His own. It is just this St. Paul means when he says that we should fill up those things that are wanting to the sufferings of Christ. This does not mean our Lord on the cross did not suffer all He could. It means rather that the physical historical Christ suffered all He could in His own human nature, but that the Mystical Christ, which is Christ and us, has not suffered to *our* fullness. All the other good thieves in the history of the world have not yet admitted their wrong and pleaded for remembrance. Our Lord is now in heaven. He therefore can suffer no more in His human nature but He can suffer more in our human natures. And so He reaches out to other human natures, to yours and mine, and asks us to do as the thief did, namely to incorporate ourselves to Him on the Cross, that sharing in His Crucifixion we might also share in His Resurrection, and that made partakers of His cross we might also be made partakers of His glory in heaven.

As our Blessed Lord on that day chose the thief as the small Host of Sacrifice, he chooses us today as the other small hosts united with Him on the Paten of the altar. Go back in your mind's eye to a Mass, to any Mass which was celebrated in the first centuries of the Church, before civilization became completely financial and economic. If we went to the Holy Sacrifice in the early Church, we would have brought to the altar each morning some bread and some wine. The priest would have used one piece of that unleavened bread and some of that wine for the sacrifice of the Mass. The rest would have been put aside, blessed, and distributed to the poor. Today we do not bring bread and wine. We bring its equivalent; we bring that which buys bread and wine. Hence the offertory collection.

Now, why do we bring bread and wine or its equivalent to the Mass? We bring bread and wine because these two things, of all things in nature, most represent the substance of life. Wheat is as the very marrow of the ground, and the grapes its very blood, both of which give us the marrow and blood of life. In bringing those two things, which give us life, nourish us, *we are equivalently bringing ourselves* to the Sacrifice of the Mass. We are therefore present at each and every Mass under the appearance of bread and wine, which stand as symbols of our body and blood. We are not passive spectators as we might be watching a spectacle in a theatre, but we are co-offering our Mass with Christ. If any picture adequately describes our role in this drama it is this: There is a great cross before us on which is stretched the great Host, Christ. Round about the hill of Calvary are our small crosses on which we, the small hosts, are to be offered. When our Lord goes to His Cross we go to our

THE PRODIGAL WORLD

little crosses, and offer ourselves in union with Him, as a clean oblation to the Heavenly Father.

At that moment we literally fulfill to the smallest detail the Savior's command: Take up your cross daily and follow Me. And in doing so, He is not asking us to do anything He has not already done Himself. Nor is it any excuse to say: "I am a poor unworthy host." So was the thief.

Note that there were two attitudes in the soul of that thief, both of which made him acceptable to our Lord. The first was the recognition of the fact that He deserved what He was suffering, but that the sinless Christ did not deserve His Cross; in other words, he was *penitent*. The second was *faith*, faith in Him whom men rejected, but whom the thief recognized as the very King of Kings.

Upon what conditions do we become small hosts in the Mass? How does our sacrifice become one with Christ's and as acceptable as the thief's? Only by reproducing in our souls the two attitudes in the soul of the Thief: *penitence* and *faith*.

First of all we must be penitent with the thief and say: "I deserve punishment for my sins. I stand in need of sacrifice." Some of us do not know how wicked or how ungrateful to God we are. If we did, we would not complain so about the shocks and pains of life. Our consciences are like darkened rooms from which light has been long excluded. We draw the curtain, and lo! everywhere before we thought was cleanliness, we find dust. Only a conscience that has been filmed over with excuses prays the prayer of the Pharisee: "I thank Thee, O God, that I am not as the rest of men." They blaspheme the God of heaven for their pain and sins and they repent not. The World War was meant to be a purgation of evil; it was meant to teach us that we cannot get along without God, but the world refused to learn the lesson. Like the thief on the left, it refuses to be penitent: it refuses to see any relation of justice between sin and sacrifice, between rebellion and a cross. But the more penitent we are, the less anxious we are to escape our cross. The more we see ourselves as we are, the more we say with the good thief: "I deserved this cross." He did not want to be excused; he did not want to have his sin explained away; he did not want to be let off; He did not ask to be taken down. He wanted only to be forgiven. He was willing even to be a small host on his own little cross—but that was because he was penitent. Nor is there given to us any other way to become little hosts with Christ in the Mass, than breaking our hearts with sorrow; for unless we admit we are wounded how can we feel the need of healing? Unless we are sorry for our part in the Crucifixion, how could we ever ask to be forgiven its sin?

The second condition of becoming a host in the offertory of the Mass is *faith*. The thief looked upon our Blessed Lord and he saw a sign above His head which read: "KING."

THE PRODIGAL WORLD

Queer king that! For a crown: thorns. For royal purple: His own blood. For a throne: a cross. For courtiers: executioners. For a coronation: a crucifixion. And yet beneath all that dross the thief saw the gold; amidst all those blasphemies he prayed.

And his faith was so strong he was content to remain on his cross. The thief on the left asked to be taken down, but not the thief on the right. Why? Because he knew there were greater evils than crucifixions, and another life beyond the cross. He had faith in the Man on the central cross who could have turned thorns into garlands and nails into rosebuds if He willed; he had faith in a Kingdom beyond the Cross, knowing that the sufferings of this world are not worthy to be compared with the joys that are to come. With the Psalmist his soul cried: "Though I should walk in the midst of the shadow of death I will fear no evils, for thou art with me."

Such faith was like that of the three youths in the fiery furnace who were commanded by the king, Nebuchadnezzar, to adore the golden statue. Their answer was: "For behold our God, whom we worship, is able to save us from the furnace of burning fire, and to deliver us out of thy hands, O king. But if He will not, be it known to thee, O king, that we will not worship thy gods, nor adore the golden statue which thou hast set up"—note that they did not ask God to deliver them from the fiery furnace, though they knew God could do it—for He "is able to save us from the furnace of burning fire." They left themselves wholly in God's hands, and like Job trusted Him though they were slain. So likewise with the good thief: He knew our Lord could deliver Him. But *He did not ask to be taken down from the cross*, for our Lord did not come down Himself even though the mob challenged Him. The thief would be a small host, if need be, unto the very end of the Mass. This did not mean the thief did not love life: He loved life as much as we love it. He wanted life, and a long life, and he found it, for what life is longer than Life Eternal? To each and every one of us in like manner it is given to discover that Eternal Life. But there is no other way to enter it than by penance and by faith which unite us to that Great Host—the Priest and Victim Christ…Thus do we become Spiritual Thieves, and steal heaven once again.

THE THIRD WORD

DELIVERED ON MARCH 15, 1936

"Woman, behold thy son... Behold thy mother."
(JOHN 19:26-27)

FIVE DAYS AGO our Blessed Lord made a triumphal entry into the City of Jerusalem: Triumphant cries rang about His ears and palms dropped beneath His feet, as the air resounded with Hosannas to the Son of David and praises to the Holy One of Israel. And to those who would have silenced the demonstration in His honor, our Lord reminds them that if their voices were silent, even the very stones would have cried out. That was the birthday of Gothic Cathedrals.

They did not know the real reason they were calling Him Holy; they did not even understand why He accepted the tribute of their praise. They thought that they were proclaiming Him a kind of earthly king. But He accepted their demonstration because He was going to be the King of a Spiritual Empire. He accepted their tributes, their hosannas, their paeans of praise, because He was going to His cross as

FULTON J. SHEEN

a Victim. And every Victim must be holy—*Sanctus, Sanctus, Sanctus*. Five days later came the *Sanctus* of the Mass of Calvary. They could say *Sanctus* to Him, for He was Holy with the Holiness of God. But at the *Sanctus* of His Mass, He does not say "Holy"—He spoke *to* the Holy ones; He does not whisper "Sanctus"—He addresses Himself *to* saints, to His Sweet Mother Mary, and His beloved disciple, John.

Striking words they are: "Woman, behold thy son… (Son) behold thy mother." He was speaking now to Saints. He had no need of saintly intercession, for he was the Holy One of God. But *we* have need of holiness, for every victim of the Mass must be holy, undefiled, and unpolluted. But how can we be holy participants in the Sacrifice of the Mass? He gave the answer; namely, by putting ourselves under the protection of His Blessed Mother. He addresses the Church and all its members in the person of John, and says to each of us: "Behold thy mother." That is why He addressed Her not as "Mother" but as "Woman." She had a universal mission, to be not only His Mother, but to be the Mother of all Christians. She had been His mother; now she was to be the Mother of His Mystical Body, the Church. And we are to be her children.

There is a tremendous mystery hidden in that one word "Woman." It was really the last lesson in detachment which Jesus had been teaching her these many years, and the first lesson of the new attachment. Our Lord had been

THE PRODIGAL WORLD

gradually alienating, as it were, His affections from His Mother; not in the sense that she was to love Him less, or that He was to love her less, but only in the sense that she was to love *us* more. She was to be detached from motherhood in the flesh, only to be more attached to that greater motherhood in the spirit—hence the word "Woman." She was to make us *other Christs*, for as Mary had raised the Holy One of God, so only she could raise us as holy ones for God, worthy to say *Sanctus, Sanctus, Sanctus* in the Mass of that prolonged Calvary.

The story of the preparation for her role as Mother of the Mystical Body of Christ is unfolded in three scenes in the Life of Her Divine Son, each one suggesting the lesson which Calvary itself was to reveal; namely, that she was called to be not only the Mother of God, but also the Mother of men; not only the Mother of Holiness, but the Mother of those who ask to be holy.

The first scene took place in the Temple where Mary and Joseph found Jesus after a three day search. The Blessed Mother reminds Him that their hearts were broken with sorrow during the long search, and He answers: "Did you not know that I must be about my Father's business?" Here He was equivalently saying: "I have another business, Mother, than the business of the Carpenter Shop. My Father has sent me into this world on the supreme business of Redemption, to make all men adopted sons of my

FULTON J. SHEEN

Heavenly Father in the greater Kingdom of the Brotherhood of Christ, Thy Son." How far the full vision of these words dawned upon Mary, we know not; whether she then understood that the Fatherhood of God meant that she was to be the Mother of men, we know not. But certainly, eighteen years later, in the second scene, the marriage feast of Cana, she came to a fuller understanding of that mission.

Let me throw in parenthetically: What a consoling thought it is, to think that our Blessed Lord, who talked penance, who preached mortification, who insisted upon taking up the cross daily and following Him, should have begun public life by assisting at a wedding festival! What a beautiful understanding of our hearts!

But to return to the point—when in the course of the banquet the wine was exhausted, Mary, always interested in others, was the first to notice and the first to seek relief from the embarrassment. She simply said to our Blessed Lord: "They have no wine." And our Blessed Lord said to her: "Woman, what is that to me and to thee? My hour is not yet come." "Woman, what is that to me?" He did not call her "Mother," but "Woman"—the same title she was to receive three years later. He was equivalently saying to her: "You are asking me to do something which belongs to me as the Son of God. You are asking me to work a miracle which only God can work; you are asking me to exercise my Divinity which has relationship to all mankind, namely as

THE PRODIGAL WORLD

its Redeemer. But once that Divinity operates for the salvation of the world, you become not only my Mother, but the Mother of redeemed humanity. Your physical motherhood passes into the wider world of spiritual motherhood, and for that reason I call you Woman." And in order to prove that her intercession is powerful in that role of universal motherhood, He ordered the pots filled with water, and in the language of Crashaw the first miracle was worked: "the conscious waters saw their God and blushed."

The third scene happens two years later. One day as our Lord was preaching someone interrupted His discourse to say, "Thy mother...stands without, seeking thee." Our Blessed Lord said, "Who is my mother?" and stretching forth His hands toward His Disciples He said: "Behold my mother and my brethren. For whosoever shall do the will of my Father, that is in heaven, he is my brother, and my sister, and mother." The meaning was unmistakable: There is such a thing as spiritual maternity; there are other bonds than those of the flesh; there are other ties than the ties of blood, namely spiritual ties which bind together those of the Kingdom where reign the Fatherhood of God and the Brotherhood of Christ.

These three scenes have their climax at the Cross where Mary is called "Woman." It was the second Annunciation. The angel said to her in the first: "Hail, Mary." Her Son speaks to her in the second: "Woman." This did not mean

FULTON J. SHEEN

she ceased to be His Mother; she is always the Mother of God; but her Motherhood enlarged and expanded; it became spiritual, it became universal, for at that moment she became *Our Mother*. Our Lord created the bond where it did not exist by nature, as only He could do.

And how did she become the mother of men? By becoming not only the mother, but also the spouse of Christ. He was the new Adam, she is the new Eve. And as Adam and Eve brought forth their natural progeny, which we are; so Christ and His Mother brought forth at the cross their spiritual progeny, which we are: children of Mary, or members of the Mystical Body of Christ. She brought forth her First-born at Bethlehem. Note that St. Luke calls our Lord the *First-born*—not that our Blessed Mother was to have other children *according to the flesh*, but only because she was to have other children *according to the spirit*. That second when our Blessed Lord said to her, "Woman," she became in a certain sense the spouse of Christ and she brought forth in sorrow her first-born in the spirit, in the pains of childbirth, and his name was John. Who the second-born was we know not. It might have been Peter. It might have been Andrew. But we at any rate are the millionth-and-millionth-born of that woman at the foot of the cross. It was a poor exchange indeed, receiving the son of Zebedee in place of the Son of God. But surely *our* gain was greater, for while she acquired but undutiful and often

THE PRODIGAL WORLD

rebellious children, we obtained the most loving Mother in the world—the Mother of Jesus.

We are children of Mary—literally, *children*. She is our Mother, not by title of fiction, not by title of courtesy; she is our mother because she endured at that particular moment the pains of childbirth for all of us. And why did our Lord give her to us as Mother? Because He knew *we could never be holy without her*. He came to us through her purity, and only through her purity can we go back to Him. There is no *Sanctus* apart from Mary. Every victim that mounts that altar under the species of bread and wine, must have said the Confiteor, and become a holy victim—but there is no holiness without Mary.

Note that when that word was spoken to our Blessed Mother, there was another woman there who was prostrated. Have you ever remarked that practically every traditional representation of the Crucifixion always pictures Magdalene on her knees at the foot of the crucifix? But you have never yet seen an image of the Blessed Mother prostrate? No. Why? Because John was there and he tells in his Gospel that she stood. He saw her stand. But why did she stand? She stood to be of service to us. She stood to be our minister, our mother.

If Mary could have prostrated herself at that moment as Magdalene did, if she could only have wept, her sorrow would have had an outlet. The sorrow that cries is never the sorrow that breaks the heart. It is the heart that can find no outlet in the fountain of tears which cracks; it is the heart that cannot have an emotional break-down that breaks. And all that sorrow was part of our purchase price paid by our Co-Redemptrix, Mary the Mother of God!

Because our Lord willed her to us as our Mother, He left her on this earth after he ascended into Heaven, in order that she might mother the infant Church. The infant Church had need of a mother, just as the infant Christ. She had to remain on earth until her family had grown. That is why we find her on Pentecost abiding in prayer with the Apostles, awaiting the descent of the Holy Ghost. She was mothering the Mystical Body of Christ.

Now she is crowned in heaven as Queen of Angels and Saints, turning heaven into another Marriage Feast of Cana when she intercedes with her Divine Savior in behalf of us, her other children, brothers of Christ and sons of the Heavenly Father. Virgin Mother! What a beautiful conjunction of Virginity and Motherhood, one supplying the defect of the other. Virginity alone lacks something: there is an incompleteness about it; something unfulfilled; a faculty unused. Motherhood alone loses something: there is a surrender, an unflowering, a plucking of a blossom. Oh! for a *rapprochement* in which there would be a Virginity that never lacked anything, and a Motherhood that never lost anything! We have both in Mary, the Virgin Mother:

THE PRODIGAL WORLD

Virgin by the overshadowing of the Holy Spirit in Bethlehem and Pentecost; Mother by the millions of her progeny from Jesus unto you and me.

There is no question here of confusing our Lady and our Lord; we venerate our Mother, we worship our Lord. We ask of Jesus those things which only God can give: Mercy, Grace, Forgiveness. We ask that Mary should intercede for us with Him, and especially at the hour of our death. Because of her nearness to Jesus which her vocation involves, we know our Lord listens especially to her appeal. To no other saint can we speak as a child to its mother: no other Virgin, or Martyr, or Mother, or Confessor, has ever suffered as much for us as she; no one has ever established better claim to our love and patronage than she. As the Mediatrix of all graces, all favors come to us from Jesus through her, as Jesus himself came to us through her. We wish to be holy, but we know there is no holiness without her, for she was the gift of Jesus to us at the *Sanctus* of His Cross. No woman can ever forget the child of her womb; then certainly Mary can never forget us. That is why we feel way down deep in our hearts, that every time she sees another innocent child at the First Communion rail, or another penitent sinner making his way to the Cross, or another broken heart pleading that the water of a wasted life be changed into the wine of God's love, that she hears once again that Word: "Woman, behold thy son."

THE FOURTH WORD

DELIVERED ON MARCH 22, 1936

"My God, my God, why hast thou forsaken me."
(MATTHEW 27:46)

THE FOURTH WORD is the Consecration of the Mass of Calvary. The first three Words were spoken to men, but the last four were spoken to God. We are now in the final stage of the Passion. In the fourth word, in all the universe, there is but God and Himself. This is the hour of darkness. Suddenly out of its blackness, the silence is broken by a cry—so terrible, so unforgettable, that even those who did not understand the dialect remembered the strange tones: "*Eloi, Eloi, lamma sabacthani.*" They recorded it so, a rough rendering of the Hebrew, because they could never get the sound of those tones out of their ears all the days of their life.

The darkness which was covering the earth at that moment was only the external symbol of the dark night of the soul within. Well indeed might the sun hide its face, at the terrible crime of deicide. The only reason the earth was

THE PRODIGAL WORLD

ever made was to have a cross erected upon it. And now that the cross was erected, creation felt the pain and went into darkness.

But why the cry of darkness? Why the cry of abandonment: "My God, my God, why hast thou forsaken me?" It was the cry of atonement for sin. What is sin? Sin is the abandonment of God by man; it is the creature forsaking the Creator, as a flower might abandon the sunlight which gave it strength and beauty. Sin is a separation, a divorce— the original divorce from unity with God, whence all other divorces are derived.

Since He came on earth to redeem man from sin, it was therefore fitting He *feel* that abandonment, that separation, that divorce. He felt it first internally, in His soul, as the base of a mountain, if conscious, might feel abandoned by the sun when a cloud drifted about it, even though its great heights were radiant with light. There was no sin in His soul, but since He willed to feel the effect of sin, an awful sense of isolation and loneliness crept over Him—the loneliness of being without God.

Surrendering the divine consolation which might have been His, He sank into an awful human aloneness, to atone for the solitariness of a soul that has lost God by sin, for the loneliness of the atheist who says there is no God, for the isolation of the man who gives up his faith for things, and for the broken-heartedness of all sinners that are homesick without God. He even went so far as to redeem all those who will not trust, who in sorrow and misery curse and abandon God, crying out: "Why this death? Why should I lose my mother? Why should I suffer? Why should I lose my property?" And He atoned for all these things by asking a "Why" of God.

But in order better to reveal the intensity of that feeling of abandonment, He revealed it by an external sign. Because man had separated himself from God, He, in atonement, permitted His Blood to be separated from His Body. Sin had entered into the blood of man; and as if the sins of the world were upon Him, He drains the chalice of His Body of His Sacred Blood. We can almost hear Him say: "Father, this is my Body; this is my Blood. They are being separated from one another as humanity has been separated from Thee. This is the consecration of my Mass."

What happened there on the Cross that day is happening now in the Mass, with this difference: On the Cross the Savior was alone; in the Mass He is with us. Our Lord is now in heaven at the right hand of the Father, making intercession for us. He therefore can never suffer again in His human nature. How then can the Mass be the re-enactment of Calvary? How can Christ renew the Cross? He cannot suffer again *in His own human nature* which is in heaven enjoying beatitude, but He can suffer again *in our human natures*. He cannot renew Calvary in His *physical*

THE PRODIGAL WORLD

body, but He can renew it in His *Mystical Body*, the Church. The Sacrifice of the Cross can be re-enacted provided we give Him our body and our blood, and give it to Him so completely that as His own, He can offer Himself anew to His Heavenly Father for the redemption of His Mystical Body, the Church.

And so the Christ goes out into the world gathering up other human natures who are willing to be Christs. In order that our sacrifices, our sorrows, our Golgothas, our Crucifixions, may not be isolated, disjointed, and unconnected, the Church collects them, harvests them, unifies them, coalesces them, masses them, and this massing of all our sacrifices of our individual human natures united with the Great Sacrifice of Christ on the Cross is the Mass.

When we assist at the Mass we are not just individuals of the earth or solitary units, but living parts of a great spiritual order in which the Infinite penetrates and enfolds the finite, the Eternal breaks into the temporal, and the Spiritual clothes itself in the garments of materiality. Nothing more solemn exists on the face of God's earth than the awe-inspiring moment of Consecration; for the Mass is not a prayer, nor a hymn, nor something said—it is a Divine Act with which we come in contact at a given moment of time. An imperfect illustration may be drawn from the radio. The air is filled with symphonies and speech. We do not put the words or music there; but, if we choose, we may establish contact with them by tuning in our radio. And so with the Mass. It is a singular, unique, Divine Act with which we come in contact each time it is re-presented and re-enacted in the Mass.

When the dye of a medal or coin is struck, the medal is the material, visible representation of a spiritual idea existing in the mind of the artist. Countless reproductions may be made from that original as each new piece of metal is brought in contact with it, and impressed by it. Despite the multiplicity of coins made, the pattern is always the same. In like manner in the Mass, the Pattern—Christ's Sacrifice on Calvary—is renewed on our altars as each human being is brought in contact with it at the moment of consecration; but the Sacrifice is one and the same despite the multiplicity of Masses. The Mass then is the communication of the Sacrifice of Calvary to us under the species of bread and wine.

We are on the altar under the appearance of bread and wine, for both are the sustenance of life therefore in giving that which gives us life we are symbolically giving ourselves. Furthermore, wheat must be ground to become bread; grapes must pass through the wine-press to become wine. Hence both are representative of Christians who are called to suffer with Christ, that they may also reign with Him.

As the consecration of the Mass draws near our Lord

is equivalently saying to us: "You, Mary; you, John; you, Peter; and you, Andrew—you, all of you—give me your body; give me your blood. Give me your whole self! I can suffer no more. I have passed through my cross, I have filled up the sufferings of my physical body, but I have not filled up the sufferings wanting to my Mystical Body, in which you are. The Mass is the moment when each one of you may literally fulfill my injunction: 'Take up your cross and follow me.'"

On the cross our Blessed Lord was looking forward to you, hoping that one day you would be giving yourself to Him at the moment of consecration. Today, in the Mass, that hope our Blessed Lord entertained for you is fulfilled. When you assist at the Mass He expects you now actually to give Him yourself.

Then as the moment of consecration arrives, the priest in obedience to the words of our Lord, "Do this for a commemoration of me," takes bread in his hands and says "This is my body"; and then over the chalice of wine says, "This is the chalice, the new testament in my blood." He does not consecrate the bread and wine together, but separately. The separate consecration of the bread and wine is a symbolic representation of the separation of body and blood, and since the Crucifixion entailed that very mystery, Calvary is thus renewed on our altar. But Christ, as has been said, is not alone on our altar; we are with Him. Hence the words of consecration have a double sense; the primary signification of the words is: "This is the Body of Christ; this is the Blood of Christ"; but the secondary signification is: "This is my body; This is my blood."

Such is the purpose of life! To redeem ourselves in union with Christ; to apply His merits to our souls by being like Him in all things, even to His Death on the Cross. He passed through His consecration on the Cross, that we might now pass through ours in the Mass. There is nothing more tragic in all the world than wasted pain. Think of how much suffering there is in hospitals, among the poor, and the bereaved. Think also of how much of that suffering goes to waste! How many of those lonesome, suffering, abandoned, crucified souls are saying with our Lord at the moment of consecration: "This is my body, take it"? And yet that is what we all should be saying at that second: "Here is my body, take it. Here is my blood, take it. Here is my soul, my will, my energy, my strength, my property, my wealth—all that I have. It is Yours. Take it! Consecrate it! Offer it! Offer it with Thyself to the Heavenly Father in order that He, looking down on this great Sacrifice, may see only Thee, His Beloved Son in whom He is well pleased. Transmute the poor bread of my life into Thy Divine Life; thrill the wine of my wasted life into Thy Divine Spirit; unite my broken heart with Thy Heart; change my cross into a Crucifix. Let not my abandonment and my sorrow and my bereavement go to waste. Gather up the fragments, and as the drop of water is absorbed by the wine at the offertory of the Mass, let my life be absorbed in Thine; let my little cross be entwined with Thy Great Cross so that I may purchase the Joys of everlasting Happiness in union with Thee.

"Consecrate these trials of my life which would go unrewarded unless united with Thee; transubstantiate me so that like bread which is now Thy Body, and wine which is now Thy Blood, I too may be wholly Thine. I care not if the species remain, or that like the bread and wine I seem to all earthly eyes the same as before. My station in life, my routine duties, my work, my family—all these are but the species of my life which may remain unchanged; but the *substance* of my life, my soul, my mind, my will, my heart, transubstantiate them, transform them wholly into Thy service, so that through me all may know how sweet is the Love of Christ."

THE FIFTH WORD

DELIVERED ON MARCH 29, 1936

"I thirst."
(JOHN 19:28)

OUR BLESSED LORD reaches the communion of His Mass when out from the depths of the Sacred Heart there wells the cry: "I thirst." This was certainly not a thirst for water, for the earth is His and the fullness thereof; it was not a thirst for any of the refreshing draughts of earth for He shut up the seas with doors when they burst forth as issuing out of a womb. And when they offered Him a drink, He took it not. It was another kind of thirst which tortured Him. He was thirsty for the souls and hearts of men. The cry was a cry for communion—the last in a long series of shepherding calls in the quest of God for men. The very fact that it was expressed in the most poignant of all human sufferings, namely, thirst, was the measure of its depth and intensity.

Men may *hunger* for God, but God *thirsts* for men. He thirsted for man in Creation as He called Him to fellowship

THE PRODIGAL WORLD

with Divinity in the Garden of Paradise; He thirsted for man in Revelation, as He tried to win back his erring heart by telling the secrets of His love; He thirsted for man in the Incarnation, when He became like the one He loved, in all things save sin. Now He was thirsting for man in Redemption, for greater love than this no man hath, that he lay down his life for his friends. It was the final appeal for communion before the curtain rang down on the Great Drama of His earthly life. All the myriad loves of parents for children, of spouse for spouse, if compacted into one great love, would have been the smallest fraction of God's love for man in that cry of thirst. It signified at once, not only how much He thirsted for the little ones, for hungry hearts and empty souls, but also His desire to satisfy our deepest longing. Really, there should be nothing mysterious in our hunger for God, for does not the hart pant after the fountain, and the sunflower turn to the sun, and the rivers run into the sea? But that He should love us, considering our own unworthiness, and how little our love is worth—*that is the mystery*! And yet such is the meaning of God's thirst for communion with us. He had already expressed it in the Parable of the Lost Sheep, when He said He was not satisfied with the ninety-nine; only the lost sheep could give Him perfect joy. Now the truth was expressed again from the cross: Nothing could adequately satisfy His thirst but the heart of every man, woman, and child, who were made for Him, and therefore could never be happy until they found their rest in Him.

The basis of this plea for communion is love, for love by its very nature tends to unity. Love of citizens one for another begets the unity of the state. Love of man and woman begets the unity of two in one flesh. The love of God for man therefore calls for a unity based upon the Incarnation, namely, the unity of all men in the Body and Blood of Christ. In order therefore that God might seal His love for us, He gave Himself to us in Holy Communion, so that as He and His human nature taken from the womb of the Blessed Mother were one in the unity of His Person, so He and we taken from the womb of humanity might be one in the unity of the Mystical Body of Christ. Hence, we use the word "receive," when speaking of communion with our Lord in the Eucharist, for literally we do "receive" Divine Life, just as really and truly as a babe receives the life of its mother. All life is sustained by communion with a higher life. If the plants could speak they would say to the moisture and sunlight: "Unless you enter into communion with me, become possessed of my higher laws and powers, you shall not have life in you." If the animals could speak, they would say, to the plants: "Unless you enter into communion with me, you shall not have my higher life in you." We say to all lower creation: "Unless you enter into communion with me, you shall not share in my human life."

THE PRODIGAL WORLD

Why then should not our Lord say to us: "Unless you enter into communion with Me, you shall not have life in you"? The lower is transformed into the higher, plants into animals, animals into man, and man, in a more exalted way, becomes "divinized" through and through by the life of Christ.

Communion then is first of all the receiving of Divine Life, a life to which we are no more entitled than marble is entitled to bloom. It is a pure gift of an All-Merciful God who so loved us that He willed to be united with us not in the bonds of flesh, but in the ineffable bonds of the Spirit where love knows no satiety, but only rapture and joy. And Oh! how quickly we should have forgotten Him could we not, like Bethlehem and Nazareth, receive Him into our souls! Neither gifts nor portraits take the place of the beloved one. And our Lord knew it well. We needed Him, and so He gave us Himself.

But there is another aspect of Communion of which we but rarely think; namely, communion implies not only *receiving* Divine Life, it means also *giving* God human life! All love is reciprocal. There is no one-sided love, for love by its nature demands mutuality. God thirsts for us, but that means that man must also thirst for God. But do we ever think of Him receiving communion from us? Every time we go to the Communion rail we say we "receive" communion, and that is all I suppose many of us do—just "receive

FULTON J. SHEEN

Communion." There is another aspect to Communion than receiving Divine Life, of which St. John speaks. St. Paul gives us the complementary truth in his Epistle to the Corinthians. Communion is not only an incorporation to the *Life* of Christ; it is also an incorporation to His *Death*. "As often as you shall eat this bread, and drink the chalice, you shall show the death of the Lord, until He come."

Natural life has two sides; the anabolic and the catabolic. The supernatural also has two sides: the building up of the Christ-pattern and the tearing down of the old-Adam. Communion therefore implies not only a "receiving" but also a "giving." There can be no ascent to a higher life without death to a lower one. Does not an Easter Sunday presuppose a Good Friday? Does not all love imply mutual self-giving which ends in self-recovery? This being so, should not the Communion rail be a place of exchange, instead of a place of exclusive receiving? Is all the *Life* to pass from Christ to us and nothing to go back in return? Are we to drain the chalice and contribute nothing to its filling? Are we to receive the bread without giving wheat to be ground, to receive the wine and give no grapes to be crushed? If all we did during our lives was to go to Communion to receive Divine Life, to take it away and leave nothing behind, we would be parasites on the Mystical Body of Christ.

The Pauline injunction bids us fill up in our body the

THE PRODIGAL WORLD

sufferings wanting to the Passion of Christ. We must therefore bring a spirit of sacrifice to the Eucharistic table; we must bring the mortification of our lower self, the crosses patiently borne, the crucifixion of our egotisms, the death of our concupiscence, and even the very difficulty of our coming to Communion. Then does Communion become what it was always intended to become, namely a Commerce between Christ and the soul, in which we give His Death shown forth in our lives, and He gives His Life shown forth in our adopted sonship. We give Him our time; He gives us His eternity. We give Him our humanity; He gives us His divinity. We give Him our nothingness; He gives us His all.

Do we really understand the nature of love? Have we not sometimes in great moments of affection for a little child, said in language which might vary from this, but which expresses the idea, "I love that child so much, I should just like to possess it within myself." Why? Because all love craves for unity. In the natural order, God has given great pleasures to the unity of the flesh. But those are nothing compared to the pleasure of the unity of the spirit, when divinity passes out to humanity, and humanity to divinity—when our will goes to Him, and He comes to us, so that we cease to be men and begin to be children of God.

Why, if there has ever been a moment in your life when a fine, noble affection made you feel as if you had been lifted into the third or the seventh heaven; if there has ever been a time in your life when a noble love of a fine human heart cast you into an ecstasy; if there has ever been a time when you have really loved a human heart—then, I ask you, think of what it must be to be united with the great Heart of Love! If the human heart in all of its fine, noble, Christian riches can so thrill, can so exalt, can make us so ecstatic, then what must be the great heart of Christ? Oh, if the spark is so bright, what must be the flame!

I wonder if we ever think how much Communion is bound up with Sacrifice, both on the part of our Lord and on the part of us, His poor weak creatures. The Mass makes the two inseparable: there is no Communion without a Consecration. There is no receiving the bread and wine we offer, until they have been transubstantiated into the Body and Blood of Christ. Communion is the consequence of the Calvary; namely, we live by what we slay. All nature witnesses this truth; our bodies live by the slaying of the beasts of the fields and the plants of the gardens. We draw life from their crucifixion. We slay them not to destroy, but to fulfill; we immolate them for the sake of communion. And now by a beautiful paradox of Divine Love, God makes His Cross the very means of our salvation. We have slain Him; we nailed Him there; we crucified Him. But Love in its eternal Heart willed not to be defeated. He willed to give us the very Life we slew; to give us the very Food we destroyed; to nourish us with the very Bread we buried, and the very Blood we poured forth. He made our very crime a *felix culpa*. He turned a Crucifixion into a Redemption; a Consecration into a Communion; a death into Life everlasting. And it is just that which makes man all the more mysterious! Why should he be loved is one mystery. But why should he not love in return? Why should our Lord be the Great Unloved; why should Love not be loved? Why then, whenever He says: "I thirst," do we reach Him vinegar and gall?

THE SIXTH WORD

DELIVERED ON APRIL 5, 1936

"It is finished."
(JOHN 29:30)

OUR BLESSED SAVIOR now comes to the *Ite Missa est* of His Mass, as He utters the cry of triumph: "It is finished."

The work of salvation is finished. But when did it begin? It began back in the agelessness of eternity, when God willed to make man. Ever since the beginning of the world there was a Divine Impatience to restore man to the arms of God. The Word was impatient in heaven, as the "Lamb slain from the beginning of the world." He was impatient in prophetic types and symbols, as His dying face was reflected in a hundred mirrors stretching through all Old Testament history. He was impatient to be the real Isaac carrying the wood of His sacrifice in obedience to the commands of His Heavenly Abraham. He was impatient to fulfill the mystic symbol of the Lamb of the Jewish Pasch, which was slain without a single bone of its body being broken; He was impatient to be the new Abel, slain

THE PRODIGAL WORLD

by his jealous brethren of the race of Cain, that His Blood might cry to Heaven for forgiveness. He was impatient in His mother's womb, as He saluted His precursor John; He was impatient in the Circumcision, as He anticipated His blood-shedding and received the name of "Savior"; He was impatient at the age of twelve, as He reminded His Mother that He had to be about His Father's business; He was impatient in His public life, as He said He had a baptism wherewith He was to be baptized and He was "straitened until it be accomplished." He was impatient in the Garden, as He turned His back to the consoling twelve legions of angels to crimson olive roots with His Redemptive Blood; He was impatient at His Last Supper as He anticipated, under the appearance of bread and wine, the separation of His Body and Blood. And then, impatience closed as the hour of darkness drew near at the end of that Last Supper—He sang. It was the only time He ever sang, the moment He went to His death.

It was a trivial matter for the world if the stars burned brightly, or the mountains stood as symbols of perplexity, or the hills made their tribute to valleys which gave them birth. What was important was that every single word predicted of Him should be true. Heaven and earth would not pass away until every jot and tittle had been fulfilled. There was only a little iota remaining, one tiny little jot; it was a word of David's about every prediction being fulfilled. Now that all else was fulfilled, He fulfilled that iota; He the true David quoted the prophetic David: "It is finished."

What is finished? The Redemption of man is finished. Love had completed its mission, for Love had done all that it could. There are two things Love can do. Love by its very nature tends to an incarnation, and every incarnation tends to a crucifixion. Does not all true love tend toward an incarnation? In the order of human love, does not the affection of husband and wife create from their mutual loves the incarnation of their confluent love in the form of a child? Once they have begotten their child do not they make sacrifices for it, even to the point of death? And thus their love tends to a crucifixion.

But this is just a reflection of the Divine Order, where the Love of God for man is so deep and intense that it led to an Incarnation, which found God in the form and habit of man, whom He loved. But our Lord's love for man did not stop with the Incarnation. Unlike everyone else who was ever born, our Lord came into this world not to live but to die. Death was the supreme goal He was seeking. Death interrupted the careers of great men, but it was no interruption to our Lord's; it was His crowning glory; it was the unique goal He was seeking. His Incarnation thus tended to the Crucifixion, for "greater love than this no man hath, that he lay down his life for his friends." Now that Love had run its course in the Redemption of man, Divine Love could say: "I have done all for my vineyard that I can do." Love can do no more than die. It is finished: "*Ite missa est.*"

His work is finished, but is ours? When He said "it is finished," He did not mean that the opportunities of His Life had ended; He meant that His work was done so perfectly that nothing could be added to it to make it more perfect—but with us, how seldom that is true. Too many of us *end* our lives but few of us see them *finished*. O, sinful life may end, but a sinful life is never a finished life.

If our lives just "end," our friends will ask: "How much did he leave?" But if our life is "finished" our friends will ask: "How much did he take with him?" A finished life is not measured by years but by deeds; not by the time spent in the vineyard, but by the work done. In a short time a man may fulfill many years; even those who come at the eleventh hour may finish their lives; even those who come to God like the thief at the last breath, may finish their lives in the Kingdom of God. Not for them the sad word of regret: "Too late, O ancient Beauty, have I loved Thee."

Our Lord finished His work, but we have not finished ours. He pointed the Way, we must follow. He laid down the Cross at the finish, but we must take it up. He finished Redemption in His Physical Body, but we have not finished it in His Mystical Body. He has finished Salvation, we have not yet applied it to our souls. He has finished the Temple, but we must live in it. He has finished the model

FULTON J. SHEEN

Cross, we must fashion ours to its pattern. He has finished sowing the seed, we must reap the harvest. He has finished filling the chalice but we have not finished drinking its refreshing draughts. He has planted the wheat fields; we must gather it into our barns. He has finished the Sacrifice of Calvary; we must finish the Mass. The Crucifixion was not meant to be an inspirational drama, but a pattern act on which we model our lives. We are not meant to sit and watch the Cross as something done and ended like the life of Socrates—*what was done on Calvary avails for us only in the degree that we repeat it in our own lives.* The Mass makes this possible, for at the renewal of Calvary on our altars we are not on-lookers but sharers in the Drama of Redemption, and there it is that we "finish" our work. He has told us: "And I, if I be lifted up from the earth, will draw all things to myself." He finished His work when He was lifted up on the Cross; we finish ours when we permit Him to draw us unto Himself in the Mass. The Mass is that which makes the Cross visible to every eye; it placards the Cross at all the cross-roads of civilization; it brings Calvary so close that even tired feet can make the journey to its sweet embrace; every hand may now reach out to touch its Sacred Burden, and every ear may hear its sweet appeal, for the Mass and the Cross are the same. In both, the same offering of a perfectly surrendered Will of the beloved Son, the same Body broken, the same Blood flowed forth, the

THE PRODIGAL WORLD

same Divine Forgiveness. All that has been said and done and acted during Holy Mass is to be taken away with us, lived, practiced, and woven into all the circumstances and conditions of our daily lives. His Sacrifice is made our sacrifice by making it the oblation of ourselves in union with Him; His Life given for us becomes our life given for Him. Thus do we go from Mass as those who have made their choice, turned their backs upon the world, and become for the generation in which we live other Christs—living, potent witnesses to the Love that died that we might live with Love.

This world of ours is full of half completed Gothic Cathedrals, of half-finished lives and half-crucified souls. Some carry the Cross to Calvary and then abandon it; others are nailed to it and detach themselves before the elevation; others are crucified, but in answer to the challenge of the world, "Come down," they come down after one hour... two hours...after two hours and fifty-nine minutes. Real Christians are they who persevere unto the end. Our Lord stayed until He had finished. The priest must likewise stay at the altar until the Mass is finished. He may not come down. So we must stay with the Cross until our lives are finished. Christ on the Cross is the pattern and model of a finished life. Our human nature is the raw material; our will is the chisel; God's grace is the energy and the inspiration. Touching the chisel to our unfinished nature we first cut off huge chunks of selfishness, then by more delicate chiselings we dig away smaller bits of egotism until finally only a brush of the hand is needed to bring out the completed masterpiece—a finished man made to the image and likeness of the pattern on the Cross. We are at the altar under the symbol of bread and wine; we have offered ourselves to our Lord; He has consecrated us; we must therefore not take ourselves back, but remain there unto the end, praying unceasingly, that when the lease of our life has ended the echo of the sixth word as we look back upon a life lived in intimacy with the Cross may ring out on our lips: "It is finished." And as the sweet accents of that *ite missa est* reach beyond the corridors of time and pierce the "hid battlements of eternity," the angel choirs and the white-robed army of the Church Triumphant will answer back: "*Deo gratias.*"

THE SEVENTH WORD

DELIVERED ON APRIL 10, 1936

"Father, into thy hands I commend my spirit."
(LUKE 23:46)

IT IS A BEAUTIFUL PARADOX that the Last Gospel of the Mass takes us back to the beginning, for it opens with the words "In the beginning." And such is life: the last of this life is the beginning of the next. Fittingly indeed, then, that the Last Word of our Lord was on His Last Gospel: "Father, into thy hands I commend my spirit." Like the Last Gospel of the Mass, it too takes Him back to the beginning, for He now goes back to the Father whence He came. He has completed His work. He began His Mass with the word: "Father." And He ends it with the same word.

Everything perfect, the Greeks used to say, travels in circles. Just as the great planets only after a long period of time complete their orbits, going back again to their starting points as if to salute Him who sent them on their way, so the Word Incarnate who came down to say His Mass now completes His earthly career, and goes back again to

FULTON J. SHEEN

His Heavenly Father who sent Him on the journey of the world's redemption. The Prodigal Son is about to return to His Father's House; for is He not the Prodigal Son? Thirty-three years ago He left the Father's House and the blessedness of Heaven, and came down to this earth of ours, which is a foreign country—for every country is foreign which is away from the Father's House. For thirty-three years He had been spending His substance. He spent the substance of His Truth in the Infallibility of His Church; He spent the substance of His Power in the Authority He gave to His apostles and their successors. He spent the substance of His Life in the Redemption and the Sacraments. Now every drop of it was gone, and He looks longingly back again to the Father's House, and with a loud cry throws His Spirit into His Father's arms, not in the attitude of one who was taking a plunge into the darkness, but as one who knew where He was going—to a homecoming with His Father.

In that Last Word and Last Gospel which took Him back to the Beginning of all beginnings, namely, His Father, is revealed the history and rhythm of life. The end of all things in some way is to get back to their beginnings. As the Son goes back to the Father; as Nicodemus must be born again; as the body returns to the dust—so the soul of man which came from God must one day go back to God. Death is not the end of all. The cold clod falling upon the

THE PRODIGAL WORLD

grave does not mark "finis" to the history of a man. The way he has lived in this life determines how he shall live in the next. If he has sought God during life, death will be like the opening of a cage, enabling him to use his wings to fly to the arms of the Divinely Beloved. If he has fled from God during life, death will be the beginning of an eternal flight away from Life and Truth and Love—and that is Hell. Before the Throne of God, whence we came on our earthly novitiate, we must one day go back to render an account of our stewardship. There will not be a human creature who, when the last sheaf is garnered, will not be found either to have accepted or rejected the Divine Gift of Redemption, and in accepting or rejecting it to have signed the warrant of his eternal destiny. As the sales on a cash register are recorded for the end of the day, so our thoughts, words, and deeds are recorded for the Final Judgment. If we but live in the Shadow of the Cross, death will not be an ending, but a beginning of Eternal Life; instead of a parting, it will be a meeting; instead of a going away, it will be an arriving; instead of being an end, it will be a Last Gospel a return to the beginning. As a voice whispers, "You must leave the earth," the Father's voice will say, "My child, come unto Me."

We have been sent into this world for only one purpose, namely, to assist at the Holy Sacrifice of the Mass. We are to take our stand at the foot of the Cross, and like those who stood under it the first day we are asked to declare our loyalties. God has given us the wheat and the grapes of life, and as the men who, in the Gospel, were given talents, we must show return on that Divine Gift. God has given us our lives as wheat and grapes. It is our duty to consecrate them and bring them back to God as bread and wine—transubstantiated, divinized, and spiritualized. There must be harvest in our hands after the springtime of the earthly pilgrimage. That is why Calvary is erected in the midst of us, and we are on its sacred hill. We were not made to be mere on-lookers, shaking our dice like the executioners of old, but rather to be participants in the great Drama of Redemption. If there is any way to picture Judgment in terms of the Mass, it is to picture it in the way the Father greeted His Son, namely, by looking at His hands. They bore the marks of labor, the callouses of redemption, and the scars of salvation. So too when our earthly pilgrimage is over, and we go back to the beginning, God will look at each of our hands. If our hands in life touched the Hands of His Divine Son, they will bear the same livid marks of nails; if our feet in life have trod over the same road that leads to Eternal Glory through the detour of a rocky and thorny Calvary, they too shall bear the same bruises; if our heart beat in unison with His then it too shall show the riven side which the wicked lance of jealous earth had pierced. Blessed indeed are they who carry in their Cross-marked hands the bread and wine of

THE PRODIGAL WORLD

consecrated lives signed with the sign and sealed with the seal of Redemptive Love. But woe unto them who come from Calvary with hands unscarred and white.

God grant that when life is over, and the earth is vanishing like the dream of one awakening, when eternity is flooding our souls with its splendors, we may with humble and triumphant faith re-echo the Last Word of Christ: "Father, into thy hands I commend my spirit."

And so the Mass of Christ ends. The *Confiteor* was His prayer to the Father for the forgiveness of our sins; the *Offertory* was the presentation on the paten of the Cross of the small hosts of the thief and ourselves; the *Sanctus* was His commending ourselves to Mary, the Queen of Saints; the *Consecration* was the separation of His Blood from His Body, and the seeming separation of Divinity and humanity; the *Communion* was His thirst for the souls of men; the *Ite Missa Est* was the finishing of the work of salvation; the *Last Gospel* was the return to the Father whence He came.

And now that the Mass is over, and He has commended His Spirit to the Father, He appears to give back His Body to His Blessed Mother at the foot of the Cross. Thus once again will the end be the beginning, for at the beginning of His earthly life He was nestled on her lap in Bethlehem, and now, on Calvary, He will take His place there once again.

Earth had been cruel to Him. His feet wandered after

FULTON J. SHEEN

lost sheep and we dug them with steel; His hands stretched out the Bread of Everlasting Life and we fastened them with nails; His lips spoke the Truth and we sealed them with dust. He came to give us Life and we took away His. But that was our fatal mistake. We really did not take it away. We only tried to take it away. He laid it down of Himself. Nowhere do the Evangelists say that He died. They say: "He gave up the ghost." It was a willing, self-determined relinquishment of life. It was not Death which approached Him, it was He who approached Death. That is why, as the end draws near, the Savior commands the portal of death to open unto Him in the presence of the Father. The chalice is gradually being drained of its rich red wine of salvation. The rocks of earth open their hungry mouths to drink as if more thirsty for the draughts of salvation than the parched heart of man; the earth itself shook in horror because men had erected God's Cross upon its breast. Magdalen, the penitent, as usual clings to His feet, and there she will be again Easter morn; John the priest with a face like a cast moulded out of love, listens to the beating of the Heart whose secrets He learned and loved and mastered; Mary thinks how different Calvary is from Bethlehem. Thirty-three years ago Mary looked down to His Sacred Face; now He looks down to her. In Bethlehem Heaven looked up into the face of earth; now the roles are reversed, and earth looks up into the face of Heaven—but

THE PRODIGAL WORLD

a Heaven marred by the scars of earth. He loved her above all the creatures of earth, for she was His Mother and the mother of us all. He saw her first on coming to earth; He shall see her last on leaving it. Their eyes meet, all aglow with life, speaking a language all their own. There is the rupture of a heart through a rapture of love. Then a bowed head, a broken heart. Back to the hands of God He gave pure and sinless His Spirit, in loud and ringing voice that trumpted eternal victory. And Mary stood alone a Childless Mother. Jesus is dead!

Mary looks up into His eyes which are so clear even in the face of death: "High Priest of Heaven and earth, Thy Mass is finished! Leave the Altar of the Cross and repair into Thy Sacristy. As High Priest Thou didst come forth from the Sacristy of Heaven, panoplied in the vestments of Humanity and bearing Thy Body as Bread and Thy Blood as Wine. Now the Sacrifice has been consummated. The Consecration bell has rung. Thou didst offer Thy Spirit to Thy Father, Thy Body and Thy Blood to man. There remains now nothing but the drained chalice. Enter into Thy Sacristy. Take off the garments of mortality and put on the white robes of immortality. Show Thy Hands, and Feet, and Side to Thy Heavenly Father and say: 'With these was I wounded in the house of those that love me'. Enter High Priest into Thy Heavenly Sacristy, and as Thy earthly ambassadors hold aloft the Bread and Wine do Thou show

FULTON J. SHEEN

Thyself to the Father in living intercession for earth even unto the consummation of the world. Earth has been cruel to Thee; but Thou wilt be kind to earth. Earth lifted Thee on the Cross, but now Thou shalt lift earth unto the Cross. Open the Door of the Heavenly Sacristy, O High Priest. Behold it is now we who stand at the door and knock!"

And Mary, what shall we say to Thee? "Mary, Thou art the Sacristan of the High Priest! Thou wert a Sacristan in Bethlehem when He did come to Thee as Wheat and Grapes in the crib of Bethlehem. Thou wert His Sacristan at the Cross, where He became the Living Bread and Wine through the Crucifixion. Thou art His Sacristan now, as He comes from the altar of the Cross bearing only the drained chalice of His Sacred Body. As that chalice is laid in your lap it may seem that Bethlehem has come back again, for He is once more yours. But it only seems—for in Bethlehem He was the chalice whose gold was to be tried by fire; but now at Calvary He is the chalice whose gold has passed through the fires of Golgotha and Calvary. In Bethlehem He was white as He came from the Father, now He is red as He came from me. But Thou art still His Sacristan! And as the Immaculate Mother of all hosts who go to the altar, do thou O Virgin Mary, send us there pure, and keep us pure, even unto the day when we enter into the Heavenly Sacristy of the Kingdom of Heaven, where Thou wilt be our eternal Sacristan and He our eternal Priest."

THE PRODIGAL WORLD

And you, friends of the Crucified, your High Priest has left the Cross, but He has left us the Altar. On the Cross He was alone; in the Mass He is with us. On the Cross He suffered in His Physical Body; on the altar He suffers in the Mystical Body which we are. On the Cross He was the unique Host; in the Mass we are the small hosts, and He the large host receiving His Calvary through us. On the Cross He was the wine; in the Mass, we are the drop of water united with the wine and consecrated with Him. In that sense He is still on the Cross, still saying the Confiteor with us, still forgiving us, still commending us to Mary, still thirsting for us, still drawing us unto the Father, for as long as sin remains on earth, still will the Cross remain.

> Whenever there is silence around me
> By day or by night
> I am startled by a cry.
> It came down from the cross—
> The first time I heard it.
> I went out and searched—
> And found a man in the throes of Crucifixion.
> And I said: "I will take you down,"
> And I tried to take the nails out of His Feet,
> But He said: "Let them be
> For I cannot be taken down
> Until every man, every woman, and every child

FULTON J. SHEEN

>Come together to take me down."
>And I said: "But I cannot bear your cry.
>What can I do?"
>And He said: "Go about the world—
>Tell every one that you meet
>There is a Man on the Cross."
> (Elizabeth Cheney)

THE FINDING OF THE LOST

DELIVERED ON APRIL 12, 1936

THE INCARNATION of our Blessed Lord was announced to a Virgin—Mary. But His Resurrection was announced to a converted sinner—Magdalene. And both were fitting. Only purity and sinlessness could welcome the all holy Son of God into the world, and hence Mary Immaculate met Him at the door of earth in the city of Bethlehem. But only a repentant sinner who had herself risen from the grave of sin to the newness of life in God could fittingly understand the triumph over sin. Hence not to the Virgin Mary, but to Magdalene, are the glad tidings of the Resurrection first announced. In this contrast is hidden the great truth of Easter Day: The Resurrection is for sinners. It is the final and absolute proof that our Lord has come not "to call the just, but sinners."

The fact that the Resurrection was first announced to Magdalene was already a proof that Easter is for the sinner, but the *way* in which she was chosen proves it still more. To the honor of womanhood, it must forever be said: A woman was closest to the Cross on Good Friday, the first at the tomb on Easter morn. That woman whom John alone mentions in his history of Easter morn was Mary Magdalene: "On the first day of the week, Mary Magdalene cometh early, when it was yet dark, unto the sepulcher; and she saw the stone taken away from the sepulcher. She ran, therefore, and cometh to Simon Peter, and to the other disciple whom Jesus loved, and saith to them: They have taken away the Lord out of the sepulcher, and we know not where they have laid him." One thought seemed to have absorbed her soul, that the Body of the Holy One had been lost! Not with her was it "out of sight, out of mind." She must find him! After telling Peter, she came back to the tomb weeping. "Now as she was weeping, she stooped down, and looked into the sepulcher, and she saw two angels in white, sitting one at the head, and one at the feet, where the body of Jesus had been laid. They say to her: Woman, why weepest thou? She saith to them: Because they have taken my Lord; and I know not where they have laid him." There was no terror at seeing the angels, for the world on fire could not have moved her, so much had grief mastered her soul. "When she had thus said, she turned herself back, and saw Jesus standing; and she knew not that it was Jesus. Jesus saith to her: Woman, why weepest thou? whom seekest thou?" And Saint John tells us she thought it was the gardener.

But perhaps Magdalene was not far wrong after all, for He was indeed the Heavenly Gardener. Every flower that

THE PRODIGAL WORLD

blooms was once a thought in His mind; every riot of color on a green stem owes its life to Him; every seed of grace in every soul is planted by His hand. As the new Adam He too has His Garden of Paradise to cultivate with His grace, to plant with His inspiration, to nourish with His everlasting waters.

However, when Magdalene took him to be the gardener, she of course meant the gardener of Joseph of Arimathea, whom she thought might know where the lost one could be found. And so she prostrates herself on her knees before Him and says to Jesus: "Sir, if thou hast taken him hence, tell me where thou hast laid him, and I will take him away." Poor Magdalene! Worn from Good Friday, wearied by Holy Saturday, with life dwindled to a shadow and strength worn to a thread—she would "take him away." Forever she stands as the type of love that can banish the hardest burden, and think the heaviest burden light.

"Jesus saith to her: Mary."

That voice was more startling than a clap of thunder. She once heard Jesus say He called His sheep by name. And now to that One who individualizes all the sin, sorrow, and tears in the world, and marks each soul with a personal, particular, and discriminating love, she turns and, as the red livid marks in hands and feet meet her gaze, she utters but one word "Rabboni." Christ had uttered "Mary" and all heaven was in it. It was only one word she uttered and all earth was in it: "Rabboni." After the mental midnight, this Dazzle; after hours of hopelessness, this Hope; after the search, this Discovery; after the loss, this Find. Magdalene was prepared only to shed reverential tears over the grave; what she was not prepared for was to see Him walking on the hills of the world. Yet such is the truth of Easter Day: the Resurrection of the Dead, the Triumph of the Defeated, and the Finding of the Lost; the springtime of the earth, the waking of life, the Trumpet of Resurrection blowing over the land of the living.

From that Easter Day on let no one believe he is beyond Redemption. There is nothing too far gone for salvation; there are no hopeless cases; there are no lost sheep that cannot be found; no lost coins that cannot be recovered to rejoice the finder and her neighbors; no prodigals beyond the hope of the embrace of the Father and the banquet of the fatted calf. If ever a cause in the world seemed lost, it was Good Friday night when the Redeemer was sealed in a rock with hideous wounds on hands and feet and side—and yet within three days the stone which the builders rejected was made the cornerstone of the Temple of God. If you could have seen Him standing before the Judgment seat of Pilate, forsaken, betrayed, beaten and alone: if you could have heard the mob scream "Crucify," and watched Pilate hold up his hands in the morning sun, with water dripping from them like glittering jewels; if you could have

THE PRODIGAL WORLD

seen that strong, powerful young man of thirty-three years go down to what you might have called a premature death of crucifixion—never for a moment would you have supposed that Pilate was the one who was really judged, that the victorious mob was the one which really lost the day, and that the hands which were nailed would one day bless the world. And yet such is the lesson of Easter Day—the Resurrection of the Dead, the Triumph of the Defeated, the Finding of the Lost; the springtime of the dead earth, the waking of life, the Trumpet of Resurrection blowing over the land of the living.

A dead Washington will not fight for his country; a dead Lincoln will not war for its unity; a dead Shakespeare will not sing his lyric drama; a dead lawyer will not save you from your legal woes; a dead doctor will not cure you of fever. Just as fantastic, just as shocking to common sense, seems the declaration that the Crucified Christ will rise again from the tomb, that the Buried King will walk to His Eternal Throne, that the dead sinners like Magdalene will live again. And yet such is the lesson of Easter Day—the Resurrection of the Dead, the Triumph of the Defeated, the Finding of the Lost; the Springtime of the dead earth, the waking of life, the Trumpet of Resurrection blowing over the land of the living.

Now, why cannot Easter happen again since Christ is risen? Cannot the hopeless once more have hope? Cannot

FULTON J. SHEEN

Magdalenes once more be forgiven? Cannot the prospect of Death be converted into Life? Apply this lesson of hope firstly to the modern world and secondly to your own personal lives.

Many minds regard our modern world as hopeless. It is indeed like a vast and horrible Good Friday where everything divine seems gone down to defeat. The future never seemed so completely unpredictable as it does today. Mankind seems to be in a kind of widowhood, in which a harrowing sense of desolation sweeps over it, as one who set out on life's journey in intimate comradeship with another, and then is suddenly bereft of that companion forever. There are wars and rumors of wars. Economics is a tangled mess. Communism is robbing men of their souls and a false education stealing away their faith. Lives have been made flabby with worldliness, and ill-prepared for the rigors of an enforced discipline. Platitudes abound on lips and unrealized desires embitter hearts. Everywhere there is confusion, hopelessness, and despair.

And yet there need not be such hopelessness and despair. The world seemed just as hopeless before when it crucified its Savior; and yet with all its paganism and nationalism it arose to newness and freshness of Christian life and civilization. The miracle of the Resurrection can happen again. The world may rise once more as it rose before, at least a dozen times since the advent of Christianity. But

THE PRODIGAL WORLD

let us suffer no illusions. It will not rise to peace and happiness through economic and political remedies alone; it will rise only through a spiritual regeneration of the hearts and souls of men. *The Resurrection of our Lord was not the resumption of an old life; it was the beginning of a new life.* It was the lesson of Christmas all over again; namely, the world will be saved not by social recovery but by re-birth— rebirth from the dead by the Power of Divinity in Christ.

This is the refrain which has been ringing through this radio course from the beginning: that is, we must not reconstruct our old life, we must rise to new life. There must be a new energy introduced from without, in the absence of which we must rot in our graves. Christ rose from the dead by the Power of God. It is vain for us to try to rise by any other Power. This Life and Power the Risen Savior has given to His Mystical Body the Church; His truth comes to us through His Vicar; His Life comes to us through the Sacraments; His Authority comes to us through the Episcopacy. But here is the stumbling block of the world. It may admit that by the Power of God Christ rose from the tomb, but it will not admit that that Power of the Risen Christ continues beyond that tomb. It sees the Church on its human side, made up of weak, frail creatures and therefore thinks it something to be ignored. It makes the same mistake Magdalene made the first Easter morn. She mistook the Risen Savior for the gardener; that is, for but a human thing. The world too sees the Risen Christ in His Mystical Body the Church, and takes it to be the gardener—something human and not divine. But Divinity is there as it was in the Garden the First Easter, and only that same Divinity can give hope to a hopeless world. We may yet attain our peace if we but seek not the political and the economic, but the new Life of the Kingdom of God. For such is the message of Easter Day—the Resurrection of the Dead, the Triumph of the Defeated, the Finding of the Lost; the springtime of the earth, the waking of life, the Trumpet of Resurrection blowing over the land of the living.

What is true of a despairing world is true of the individual souls in it. This earth of ours today is filled with men who have lost their way; with souls whose sins have been psychoanalyzed a thousand times, but never forgiven once; with bodies that have been embittered by pain and never sweetened by a vision of the cross; with hearts that have pursued a thousand fancies, only to be utterly disillusioned at the end; with the poor who thought riches would give them peace of mind; with the despairing who thought drink could make them forget.

But to all these souls, the Easter message rings out: There is no reason for despair. The Resurrection was announced to a Magdalene—a soul once like our own. Peace awaits you in the service of the God who made you; Certitude awaits you in Infallibility; Redemption awaits

THE PRODIGAL WORLD

you in the Mass; Pardon beckons you in the Confessional; Love desires you in the Eucharist. And all that can be yours provided you do not mistake Christ for the gardener, and think the Church which prolongs His Life is only a human thing in a dying world.

What He did to bodies during His earthly life, He is doing to souls now in His Mystical Body, the Church. Had you and I walked down the street with Him, we would have noticed that it was principally only what our modern sociologists call the dependents, the defectives, and the delinquents which interested Him. What always seemed to catch His eyes was a beggar like Lazarus lying yonder in the shadow of a rich man's door, all sores and rags and vermin, from whom the rest of men stepped back as unclean; the blind man of Jericho shrieking and shouting for light; the woman of the coast town suffering from an issue of blood; the corpse of the son of the widow of Naim; the woman taken in sin stretched in the dust welting under the gaze of the Pharisees and cringing in fear from their stones; the poor laborer with a patch on his garments; the little children who annoyed busy men. But to Him these were all citizens of a world of infinite possibilities. The old beggar was an immortal soul clean enough to nestle in the arms of Abraham; the blind man had eyes that could see Divinity which men with earthly eyes had missed; each and every one of these aimless looking creatures who seemed beyond

FULTON J. SHEEN

the power of recovery might change at any second, for the love of God was beating down on them, and under its rays these sorry grubs might become glorious, winged creatures, if they but saw in Him not the humanity of a gardener but the Divinity of the Crucified Savior, walking in the newness of life. For such is the message of Easter Day: The Resurrection of the Dead, the Triumph of the Defeated, the Finding of the Lost; the springtime of the earth, the waking of life, the Trumpet of Resurrection blowing over the land of the living.

And so in conclusion, the thought I would give to you is that no matter how hopeless things seem to be, there is still hope, for Christ is the Resurrection and the Life. He that can make snowflakes out of dirty drops of water, diamonds out of charcoal, and saints out of Magdalenes, can also make you victorious if you but confess Him in His earthly and Mystical Life as Christ the Son of the Living God.

Alfred Noyes relates in his *Unknown God* the transforming power of Christ. He says that in his early days he once dined with the poet Swinburne. Swinburne, you remember, was one of the best known anti-Christian poets of modern times; the poet who refused to give glory to God, but only to man, for "man is the master of all." During the course of a conversation about Russian atrocities the expression of Swinburne, which up to this time had been

THE PRODIGAL WORLD

kindly, suddenly changed; and like a child possessed—in the old direful sense of possession—he spat out these words: "Christianity itself never conceived anything more *ghastly*."

Many years after Swinburne's death, Noyes visited the vicinity of his old home. The gates were open and the dark winding road to Swinburne's house was strewn with ferns and flowers in two regular lanes by the hands of nuns; for the poet's old home had become a convent. And it was now the Feast of the Sacred Heart. At the door of the house a procession was forming, with long lines of children in white, and the black-robed nuns behind the fair bearers of the canopy. Then with lights and incense the priest with the Host moved slowly forward under the canopy, preceded by the procession, singing *O Salutaris Hostia* over the very same paths in which the poet had written his anti-Christian songs. Then the long procession stopped at a flower decked altar, before which all knelt for Benediction in the mellowing, scented air.

And as the hymn *Tantum Ergo* rang out, Noyes said he glanced up over the walls of the former library, which is now a chapel of the Sacred Heart, and on its window saw the initials of a former owner unchanged: I. H. S. Those of you who know what those initials mean understand the lesson of Easter: The dead may still rise from their graves!

Cardinal Hayes States Purpose of Catholic Hour
EXTRACT FROM HIS ADDRESS AT THE INAUGURAL PROGRAM
IN THE STUDIO OF THE NATIONAL BROADCASTING COMPANY
NEW YORK CITY, MARCH 2, 1930

Our congratulations and our gratitude are extended to the National Council of Catholic Men and its officials, and to all who, by their financial support, have made it possible to use this offer of the National Broadcasting Company. The heavy expense of managing and financing a weekly program, its musical numbers, its speakers, the subsequent answering of inquiries, must be met.

This radio hour is for all the people of the United States. To our fellow-citizens, in this word of dedication, we wish to express a cordial greeting and, indeed, congratulations. For this radio hour is one of service to America, which certainly will listen in interestedly, and even sympathetically, I am sure, to the voice of the ancient Church with its historic background of all the centuries of the Christian era, and with its own notable contribution to the discovery, exploration, foundation and growth of our glorious country.

Thus to voice before a vast public the Catholic Church is no light task. Our prayers will be with those who have that task in hand. We feel certain that it will have both the good will and the good wishes of the great majority of our countrymen. Surely, there is no true lover of our Country who does not eagerly hope for a less worldly, a less material, and a more spiritual standard among our people.

With good will, with kindness and with Christ-like sympathy for all, this work is inaugurated. So may it continue. So may it be fulfilled. This word of dedication voices, therefore, the hope that this radio hour may serve to make known, to explain with the charity of Christ, our faith, which we love even as we love Christ Himself. May it serve to make better understood that faith as it really is—a light revealing the pathway to heaven: a strength, and a power divine through Christ; pardoning our sins, elevating, consecrating our common every-day duties and joys, bringing not only justice but gladness and peace to our searching and questioning hearts.